Breakthrough:
Women in Law Enforcement

Elizabeth Simpson Smith

Walker and Company
New York, New York

Copyright © 1982 by Elizabeth Simpson Smith

All rights reserved. No part of this book may be reproduced or transmitted in any form or by any means, electric or mechanical, including photocopying, recording, or by any information storage and retrieval system, without permission in writing from the Publisher.

First published in the United States of America in 1982 by the Walker Publishing Company, Inc.

Published simultaneously in Canada by John Wiley & Sons
Canada, Limited, Rexdale, Ontario.

ISBN: 0-8027-6468-1

Library of Congress Catalog Card Number: 82-6978

Printed in the United States of America

10 9 8 7 6 5 4 3 2 1

Library of Congress Cataloging in Publication Data

Smith, Elizabeth Simpson.
  Breakthrough, women in law enforcement.

  Includes index.
  1. Policewomen—United States—Biography. 2. Women correctional personnel—United States—Biography. 3. Women detectives—United States—Biography. I. Title. HV8023.S62   1982   363.2' 088042   82-6978
ISBN 0-8027-6468-1   AACR2

For my nieces
Anne
Jan
Lenrae
Jocelyn
and for my godchild, Betsy

Acknowledgments

THE AUTHOR WISHES to express sincere gratitude to the following people who have assisted in research or in the preparation of this manuscript: Peggy Dixon, Betty Parker, Darlene Cook, Diana Gleasner, Kathy and Walter Schmitt, Katie Wood, Greg Huffman, Nancy Wall, Diana Bond, Mollie Taylor, Tony LaTona, Phil Flanary, Chief Leo F. Callahan, Bill Trible of the FBI, Nancy Bowman of OEO, Anthony Travisono of the American Corrections Association, Don Lawrence of Gaston College, Dennis W. Lund of NELS, Carolen Bailey of IAWP, Hattie M. Carrington of the Police Foundation, Captain Beryl Thompson, Eugene Estrada of the Los Angeles Public Library, Jim Amormino of the Los Angeles Police Department, her editor, Jeanne Gardner, Dixie Lee Nims of Florida's Department of Commerce, Steve Ford—and of course to Ed.

Contents

	Page
Foreword, by Leo F. Callahan	1
Introduction	3
Donna Marie Pence, Undercover Agent	10
Jenna Garman Sprecher, Florida Marine Patrol	29
Maureen Anne Higgins, FBI Agent	49
Priscilla Pepper Karansky, Mounted Police	63
Elizabeth Aytes (Cookie) Kandler, Correctional Superintendent	83
And Others Who Excel	
Geraldine Anderson Lawrence, Border Patrol Agent	105
Susan Marie Stanton, Jailer	110
Kathryn Harper Morris, Airport Security Agent	113
Virginia Quintana Guzman, Police Detective	116
Rae Hassell McNamara, State Director of Prisons	119
Glossary	123
Criminal Justice Educational Opportunities	125
Jobs Within the Criminal Justice System	150
Index	153

Foreword

ONE OF THE MOST REWARDING AND CHALLENGING CAreers a young woman can choose today is that of a law-enforcement officer. Police agencies throughout the United States are actively recruiting females to join their departments in numbers that will result in their being reflective in makeup of the communities they serve.

For a number of years, a career in law enforcement was virtually closed to women for several reasons. It was generally felt that a police officer's job was strictly one for large, tough males and that size and sex were criteria for success. This, of course, has proven to be a faulty premise, and size requirements as they pertained to height and weight are no longer real barriers. Concentration is now placed on mental and psychological factors, seeking those with the temperament to deal with human behavior and stress-laden situations. These attributes, which are needed to achieve success in the field of law enforcement, apply equally to men and women.

In previous years, women who were employed in police agencies were usually assigned as "police women" in such assignments as shoplifting squads, juvenile bureaus, and other similar assignments considered "nondangerous." They were not assigned to patrol-car duty or as investigating detectives.

As our times have changed, increasing awareness of uninformed or discriminatory practices, a whole new world of employment for women has opened up. Old myths and misconceptions have been, and are continuing to be, swept away. Women are beginning to play a vital and a viable role in changing the face of law enforcement in America today. They are joining police forces in slowly increasing numbers and are adding new dimensions to the role of police officer. The term "police woman" has been appropriately dropped, and they are called what they are, police officers.

I feel women bring with them some excellent traits that improve our profession. They are usually concise, methodical, and are genuinely concerned with being of help to people. They are usually good planners, know how to budget their time, and possess a lot of common sense. They use their intelligence and natural approach to compensate for what they may lack in physical stature.

Today's female police officers are assigned to patrol duties, detective divisions, undercover investigations, and all other tasks that cover the full spectrum of law enforcement. I'm proud to say that both of my daughters are police officers. They both serve as deputy sheriffs in Broward County, Florida. Carole began her career as a dispatcher. She then applied for a job as deputy sheriff and, after graduation from the Police Academy, served as a road-patrol officer, intelligence officer assigned to the Organized Crime Unit, and is now a detective working on cases that involve crimes against persons, such as aggravated assaults.

Vicki, after graduation from the Police Academy, spent some time in technical services, which involved working with fingerprint identification and photography. She then worked as a narcotics officer on airport duty and is presently assigned as an undercover narcotics investigator with the Organized Crime Unit. My wife, Carole, herself a career employee with the United States Post Office Department, where she serves as a supervisor, is very proud and supportive of our daughters' efforts in the field of public service.

So you can see that the opportunities and challenges are there. Law enforcement is an interesting and a rewarding career where one can satisfy personal goals and accomplishments while, at the same time, providing a benefit to the community in which one lives.

Break through, and accept that challenge!

LEO F. CALLAHAN,
CHIEF OF POLICE, FORT LAUDERDALE, FLORIDA
PRESIDENT, INTERNATIONAL ASSOCIATION OF
CHIEFS OF POLICE

Introduction

THE YEAR WAS 1911. A DUST-LADEN TRAIN CHUGGED INTO the station of a small coal-mining town in Pennsylvania and rattled to a halt. Alice Stebbins Wells alighted and, her dark dress brushing the ground as she walked, proceeded toward the town theater and a gathering crowd of onlookers.

Then she stopped short. Before her on the walkway in front of the theater stood a sign almost as tall as she, with bold black letters proclaiming: MRS. WELLS, FIRST POLICEWOMAN—SEE HER!

If Alice Wells hadn't possessed a keen sense of humor, she might have felt like a freak in a carnival. She had come to the town to be heard rather than seen. Forfeiting her salary and living off whatever lecture fees she managed to collect, Alice was bent on inspiring cities and towns across the country to hire female law-enforcement officers.

Only one year earlier Alice had returned from the Far East as a religious student-worker and settled in Los Angeles, California. Fired with religious zeal, she felt that police work offered the greatest opportunity for "applied Christianity," that crime could be reduced by curing social ills. And she was convinced that a female officer could best deal with children, young people and with other women.

Alice drew up a petition requesting that she be named a police officer and circulated it through Los Angeles, procuring the signatures of 100 prominent citizens. Faced with the petition, the city succumbed. And on a memorable September morning in 1910, Alice Wells became the first woman in the entire country to be sworn in as a police officer.

Alice Stebbins Wells, first policewoman to be officially sworn to duty (photo courtesy Los Angeles Police Department)

There had been women working in police departments before, but they served mainly as prison matrons and were never sworn in. Even as early as 1776, a Mary Lindsey was listed as "gaoler" (old English manner of spelling "jailer") for Henrico County, Virginia. But in colonial days, the jails were often located on private property or even in the homes of settlers, and Mary probably did little more than carry the key and dish up food.

In 1845 New York City hired the first female prison matron in the United States. And in 1893 the mayor of Chicago, Illinois, appointed Marie Owens, widow of a police officer, as a member of the force. Although Marie served for 30 years, she was never sworn in.

In 1905 Portland, Oregon, gave Lola Baldwin limited police power in cases involving women, but that city, too, failed to swear her to regular duty.

Standing a little over 5 feet tall, Alice Wells wore no uniform, carried no weapon, and usually stuffed her star-shaped badge into her pocketbook. On her first day at work, she reported to her first sergeant and found him sitting in his office in shirt sleeves. The sergeant jumped to his feet. "Either you'll have to get used to this or we will," he stuttered, scrambling into his coat.

Alice was assigned an office in a jury room on the third floor, far from the activity in the police station below. Her walls were lined with books of yellowed court records, behind which rats scurried back and forth across the shelves.

Although she moved around the city quietly, Alice began almost immediately to assert her influence. She felt picture shows were here to stay, but she insisted that they not be shown in total darkness. She campaigned to do away with movies of violence, crime and "scenes of the spicy sort." At dance halls she insisted that they discontinue their "moonlight dances" during which no lights were turned on. She visited penny arcades, skating rinks and parks in an effort to make them safe and wholesome for women and children. Even with her gentle manner and without a weapon, Alice Wells made 13 arrests during her first year of duty.

Newsreels, newspapers and magazines carried the story of Alice Wells across the country, and she became something of a celebrity. Her speaking tours began to reap results. By 1916, policewomen were serving in 25 cities covering 20 states. Two years later, 200 cities reported having women on their forces. But always their duties were limited, their chances for advancement almost nil.

Nevertheless, many of the new officers, like the women profiled in this book, became trailblazers. In 1918, the largest department of policewomen in the world was organized in Indianapolis, Indiana. With Captain Clara Burnside at its head, the 24 women wore plain clothes and worked on streets and inside stores to wipe out purse-snatching and shoplifting. They set up a court of their own and based their efficiency not on the number of arrests, as male officers did, but on the number of people "whose feet we were able to set on the right path." Their results were impressive. In 1921 these women apprehended 4,120 wrongdoers but made only 543 actual arrests. The others were counseled and set free as one-time offenders.

In 1925, Alice McCarthy joined the Chicago, Illinois, police force when her singing career fizzled. Sandy-haired, brisk and sober, Alice became one of the city's best-known cops. She patrolled the dark streets alone—and unafraid. Unlike her predecessors, she used her .38-caliber pistol when she needed it, and she killed when necessary. Alice lived alone in a South Side apartment, studied French and Italian when she wasn't working and attended mass every Sunday.

In 1935, University Heights, Iowa, was a quiet community with 2,000 residents and no law-enforcement officer. The number of petty crimes and traffic violations were mounting, and the town decided to hire a policeman. But Esther Winder, a 34-year-old wife and mother who had always yearned to be a cop, applied for the job and got it. Dressed in tight black pants and leather jacket, white crash helmet and boots, and with a pearl-handled pistol and a can of chemical mace swinging from her hips, Esther daily hopped on her Harley-Davidson motorcycle and roared through the streets. By night she preferred her battered red Studebaker for late cruising. Esther never used either the mace or the pistol, but she wrote lots of traffic tickets, and her visibility drastically reduced the rate of petty crime. When convicts escaped from a nearby prison, Esther and her bloodhound, Portia, were quick to join the search. In 1969, Esther, then a 70-year-old grandmother, turned in her badge and retired.

In 1964, Everene Cooper Johnson, a black woman, joined her father, Detective Sergeant Everett Cooper, on the Washington,

D.C., Metropolitan Police Force, thus becoming the first father-daughter team in the nation. Everene carried a Colt .38 Special and worked with purse-snatchers and in areas involving threats to young people—crowds milling around theaters, drug sellers, pimps and winos. Everene had grown up with police work, was familiar with guns and passed the sharp-shooter tests on her first attempt.

Slowly a few inroads were being made in large metropolitan areas. In 1930, Massachusetts became the first state to hire female troopers. In the late 1950's the Miami, Florida, Police Department assigned its first woman to plainclothes detective duties. But in each case the women officers were assigned duties involving either other women or children, just as Alice Wells visualized. Most of them resented this. They felt their potential was being wasted, their chance for advancement thwarted. They wanted the same duties that male officers assumed, regardless of sacrifice or danger. But the future looked bleak. In 1970, although there were 5,617 female law-enforcement officers in the country, all of them had limited authority. It took an act of Congress to improve the outlook.

In the 1970's, Congress passed a series of federal laws designed to erase discrimination. The federal government, of course, led the way in hiring women to full-fledged law-enforcement positions. In 1971, the Secret Service hired its first female agents. The Federal Bureau of Investigation (FBI) followed suit one year later.

But cities and states were lagging far behind. In 1968, Indianapolis, Indiana, had assigned two women to traffic patrol with their arrest powers extending to any violator, regardless of sex. The two officers, Betty Blankenship and Elizabeth Coffal, were assigned to Car 47 with only one day's notice and no special training. But it wasn't until four years later that states and other municipalities, forced by a federal law passed in 1972, began to open their doors. Then the 1970's became the decade for advancement in almost every field of law enforcement.

In 1972, there were only seven women on regular police-patrol duty in all the cities of our country combined. By 1975 there were 42,000 state law-enforcement officers in the United States, yet only 135 of them were women. But by 1978 there were more than 9,000 female law-enforcement officers in the nation, presumably sharing the same duties as males.

Reporting for duty required a great deal of courage from these female rookies. They discovered right off that they not only had to battle crime but they had to fight prejudice and stereotypical images starting from their first day of work. For centuries, the general conception of women was that they (1) don't fight; (2) don't carry guns; (3) don't arrest people; (4) don't make men's salaries. Police work, like war and football, was for men.

Women officers found that their male coworkers either didn't trust them and called them "super broads" or considered them social workers in uniform. The wives of some of the officers circulated petitions to prevent a woman from riding patrol with their husbands. And the families, friends and boyfriends often chided the female officers and gave them little emotional support. Even the public scoffed and greeted them with scorn.

Even today female recruits still face many of the same reactions and find that they must "think like men, work like dogs and act like ladies" to earn their credibility. As the chapters in this book indicate, the training for women is rigorous and demanding, the same training that men undergo. Yet when women emerge from the Academy ready for action and confident in their ability, they run headlong into one of their biggest problems—male chauvinism. The officers they ride patrol with often rush to open the car door or try to protect them from danger with a "you-just-sit-tight-while-I-take-care-of-this" attitude.

One officer, finding a jumper on a bridge, told his female partner, "Here, hold my hat while I rush him." The policewoman lost no time in establishing her professionalism. "Hold your own damn hat," she snapped. "This city doesn't pay me to hold your hat." And she joined the action.

The incident is small, but it reflects the attitude of today's female law-enforcement officer. She's ready for whatever is demanded of her, she asks for no special concessions and she doesn't want to be treated like a Barbie doll.

She'll even put up with minor displays of discrimination when they don't interfere with her performance. In 1973, Karen Kilroy reported for her first patrol assignment in Cleveland, Ohio. She was directed to an auto emblazoned with the slogan, "Our Men Serve All Men." Undismayed, Karen tucked her hair under her cap and set about her job. Only three nights later she gave chase to an armed hold-up man—and captured him. Cleveland's women also serve!

Comprehensive studies have dispelled the two greatest fears regarding women in law enforcement: (1) that they will panic in the face of danger and violence; (2) that they lack the necessary physical stamina.

Studies have also shown that women excel in an unexpected way. They arouse less antagonism than men when dealing with the public; they stimulate less fear and provoke less violence and abuse.

The main battlefront now is one within the organization. Female officers are often shuttled to desk jobs involving paperwork or to departments dealing only with women and juveniles. Even worse, they're often prevented from taking examinations for promotions, and few of them rise above the rank of officer. Captain Beryl A. Thompson of the Seattle, Washington, Police Department is one of the few exceptions. "We still have a long, long way to go," she says. "A young woman entering law enforcement today must be prepared to meet resistance in what will always be a male-dominated field. But the opportunity is there for those who wish to serve."

Captain Thompson cautions the young aspirant to erase from her thinking the TV image of a police officer, to come into law enforcement with her eyes open, prepared to work hard and to gain acceptance and credibility without expecting too much too soon.

Unfortunately, we live in an age of alarming crime and violence. Also unfortunately, our citizens who lay their lives on the line to make our lives safe are often treated with disrespect. Even the news media sometimes fail to give law enforcement the support it deserves.

To deal effectively with crime requires intelligence, training, stamina, dedication and a giant-size portion of courage. On these scores, both men and women are daily proving themselves equal to the challenge.

But, as Alice Wells foresaw, much emphasis is now being put on the prevention of crime and the rehabilitation of the criminal. Both areas demand special qualities—sensitivity, insight and an eagerness to help and set aright—qualities that women have for centuries been conditioned to develop. And that's where women excel.

"I don't like giving in to negative feelings. As soon as I'm told I can't do something, that's when it becomes number one in my life."

Donna Marie Pence, Undercover Agent

IT WAS THE WEEK BEFORE CHRISTMAS, 1979. DONNA Marie Pence, undercover narcotics agent with the Tennessee Bureau of Investigation, had just received a hot tip involving Sam, a prison warden at the state penitentiary. Sam was reportedly dealing in Quāālude, a highly addictive methaqualone drug, both inside prison and at his second job as salesman at a used-car lot.

The informant was specific. Sam was 6'2" tall, weighed 230 pounds and would be armed. Donna was to use the code "grand slam" to identify herself. If she played her role properly she'd be able to buy some Quāālude tablets. Then she'd have hard evidence and the state could make a case.

Donna made the telephone call, used the code and set up a meeting at the used-car lot. Because her own assigned automobile looked too much like a police car, she borrowed one belonging to another agent. Carefully she cleaned out under the seats, the sun visor over the driver's seat and the glove compartment, removing all police identification. With a gun in her coat pocket and wired with a microphone so all her activities would be picked up by surveillance officers in a van parked one mile from the car lot, Donna set out on the mission.

En route she hardly noticed the gaily decorated shop windows, the plump Santas jingling their bells on street corners. Her mind was on Sam and the outcome of her meeting. Drug traffic inside the penitentiary had reached an alarming rate, and Sam was responsible for most of it. He'd be a big catch.

Donna swung into the lot and parked in the spot Sam had indicated. Also at Sam's direction, she pulled out a tube of lipstick and began applying it. Through the rearview mirror she saw him approach, a lumbering hulk of a man, hatless, his overcoat hanging loose. They exchanged a few words, the transfer was made, and Donna tucked the Quaaludes in her purse while Sam pocketed her money.

Now she had the goods on him.

But that didn't satisfy Donna. If I can get him to talk, gain his confidence, he may reveal where he gets his drugs, she thought. And that's even more important than booking Sam.

She leaned across the seat, opened the door on the passenger side. "Might as well come in out of the cold," she said.

Sam climbed in and snapped the door closed. The smell of stale tobacco smoke filled the car. Donna began a line of chatter—the weather, football scores, heavy automobile traffic on the street—anything to keep him talking. Sam began to loosen up.

"Done your Christmas shopping yet?" He peeled the wrapper from a cigar, dropped the paper to the floor.

"Nope," Donna replied. "I've got this lousy damn cold. Haven't felt like it."

Sam bit off the tip of the cigar, rummaged in his pocket for a match. "What're you doing for it?"

"Nothing." Donna applied a tissue to her nose. "My boyfriend is a real party guy. Wants to go some place every night. I don't even get any sleep."

"What's he do, this boyfriend?" Sam suddenly flipped down the sun visor over the passenger seat. A police badge fell with a thud into the middle of his lap.

They both sat stunned, silent. If Sam suspected Donna was a cop he'd "take care" of her right on the spot. Yet Donna knew they couldn't fight it out in the car. If Sam made a move she'd have to shoot right through her coat and take her chances. She slid her hand into the pocket, fingered the gun, waited for his reaction.

Then she had a second thought.

"I guess I should tell you my boyfriend is a cop," she said, controlling the quiver in her voice. "This is his car."

Slowly Sam opened the badge case, examined the photograph of the male agent inside.

"He knows I deal in grass," Donna raced on, "but he doesn't

know I'm into pills. I use his car when I deal dope because I know I won't get stopped for tickets. I'd get in a pack of trouble if he knew."

Sam ran his thumb over the badge while Donna fixed her gaze steadily on his hands. Suddenly he snapped the case shut and stuck it back under the visor.

"For a minute you had me scared," he turned sideways, looked Donna squarely in the face. "But a gal like you couldn't be no cop." He opened the door, stepped out and walked away. Donna was beginning to relax when Sam wheeled around abruptly, thrust his hand into his pocket. Donna pulled out her gun, held it low and aimed, waiting for Sam's first move.

"Want a little coke?" he called across the lot in a hoarse stage whisper.

It wasn't what she expected, but an offer of cocaine (coke) was far better than gunshots.

Donna's mind was numb as she drove to meet her surveillance team. A man like Sam didn't play games. If he'd suspected Donna he would have shot without hesitation. Yet if Donna had fired a second too soon it would be hard to convince the courts her action was in self-defense. Then her job would be in jeopardy, her

department up for criticism and censure. Later she'd mentally replay the scene time and again, questioning her own performance, trying to find ways to improve. But for the moment she was content to safely guide the car along the busy thoroughfare.

When she arrived at the meeting point, she found her back-up men in a rage.

"They were really hacked off," Donna recalls. "They wanted to know what in hell I was trying to do, making up a cop story like that. Then it dawned on me. They didn't know about the badge. I had forgotten to give them some clue on my microphone. They thought I was just trying to see how far I could string him along."

As a fruitful ending, Donna continued to "play" Sam until she engineered her way to his supplier.

The Sam incident is only one of many such cases for Donna since that August day in 1976 when she signed on with the Tennessee Bureau of Investigation as its first female agent. Less than a week later, Donna's team routed out a patch of marijuana valued at the lofty sum of $100,000. And exactly 22 months later there was a contract out on her life, a hit job just waiting for a professional killer to pick up $10,000 to wipe her out.

That's moving swiftly for a beginner. But you learn early that

Far left:
Donna disguised as a drug addict
Left: Posing as a pregnant woman often provides safety for Donna
Right:
Donna playing the role of a wino
(Photos by Chip DeVilbiss; make-up by Rick Brown)

undercover work has a double-edged clock system all its own. Most of the time the process is tedious, with slow-rolling hours of surveillance, talking, watching, spying, hoping. But once the crime is established, the action is fast. You move in quickly, make your arrests.

Donna has learned to live with both time systems. She knows firsthand what it's like to become a fictitious character, to set up residence in some drug-infested town and spend months methodically plodding along until she has accumulated enough evidence to make the first arrest. On assignment, Donna assumes a role like an actress. In Memphis she's been Tammi, exotic dancer. In Knoxville she was Dani Foster, college student. In another town she may be Corinne, waitress, or Debbie, secretary. Meanwhile, her life is on the line. She goes into bars, dark alleys, rough neighborhoods. She buys drugs with funds provided by the state and works her way up the ladder of dealers until she finally meets the head of the ring. Then it's time for the raid.

The time to come out from undercover is a decision Donna makes when she determines that no further purchases would produce additional information and she'd just be wasting taxpayers' money. Then she presents her evidence to a grand jury and a true bill is returned against the drug sellers. The roundup begins.

The bureau works with local law-enforcement officers for the showdown. Donna goes along for identification. It's her favorite role, and her choice line is "Remember me?" when she points to the drug peddler.

"The look on the faces of those jerks is priceless," Donna says. "They've been bragging to me all along about how smart they are and how stupid cops are. They always think cops are stupid. It gives me a great deal of satisfaction to drop my role and become Donna Pence, undercover agent, again."

Donna had a bit of drama training in high school and it pays off handsomely. She never considered acting as a career, but she calls herself "a great little games player."

A first glimpse of Donna is unsettling. Her appearance is about as far removed from the stereotypical gun-toting police officer as you can imagine. She has long, dark hair, milky-smooth skin and large green eyes, sometimes framed by oversize designer glasses. It's almost impossible to think of her as a target for assassination by some seasoned criminal until you hear her throaty, sensual voice slip into phrases like "under the hammer," "hit man" or "walking the scripts." She uses these telltale words as casually as an office secretary speaks of typewriter ribbons or an artist of paints.

The assignment that triggered the contract on Donna's life took place in Norwood (fictitious name), a mountain town in east Tennessee known for "taking care of its own." Law-enforcement officers in Norwood rate as high on the popularity scale as poison ivy on spring break. Its inhabitants abide by a set of unwritten laws designed to suit their own way of life. They carry guns and knives. They tolerate a climate of commerce that includes buying and selling stolen property and trafficking in drugs. The area's reputation was well known at the bureau.

In reports that filtered in, one name kept showing up—a mainliner who "walked the scripts" (writing prescriptions for pharmaceutical drugs on stolen prescription pads). The drug involved was Dilaudid, an extremely addictive and powerful pain killer. Dilaudid at the time cost the pharmacy $.11 wholesale for a four-milligram tablet but was selling on the street for $45. Junkies crumble the tablet into a syringe, add water and inject the solution into a vein for a quick rush. The effect can last from two to six hours, then the junkies are on the street again, looking for another buy, ready to steal or even kill to support their addiction. But no one in Norwood was willing to testify for fear of "being taken care of."

Then the attorney general of Tennessee informed the bureau that he had an informant, someone who would cooperate in breaking up Norwood's heinous drug ring. The informant was named Jimmy, an ex-convict under arrest again and willing to squeal to get a lighter sentence. Jimmy was said to be "good."

"A good informant is priceless," Donna says. "He can meet anybody and get to know all of them so well he can take you in."

Donna was assigned to the case.

She listened to the facts carefully, then made her own arrangements. She'd have to invent a cover story convincing enough to fool Jimmy's drug dealers. So she became Joni Martin, girlfriend of his former cellmate at the state penitentiary. She'd pretend to be job hunting in the area and would look him up. Jimmy, of course, would play his true-to-life role—pimp and street dealer in drugs.

Donna stripped her wallet of the identification cards and

photographs she normally carried—pictures of her husband and two dogs—and inserted new snapshots to fit her role. She secured a phony driver's license and credit card showing her name to be Joni Martin. She applied heavy makeup, donned a frowzy wig, put on skin-fitting tank tops and jeans and stepped into sneakers ("I always wear shoes I can run in"). For a final touch, she sprinkled her language with an abundance of "ain'ts" and earthy four-letter words.

"I actually *become* that person," Donna says. "Being able to con those creeps is like an addiction. Every time you succeed you want to try again for bigger fish."

Her addiction is accompanied by anger. At the street level, women are regarded with little value, Donna says. If a man is holding drugs and sees a police officer approach, he'll toss the package to his girlfriend and let her take the rap. A woman, he figures, will get a lighter sentence. So why not let her go to jail? Then he can remain free and continue his "business."

"That's so appalling to me that it makes me mad just to think of it," Donna adds. "Luckily it's a break for me, though. Those men have such a low opinion of women that they can't think of them as being anything other than their 'old ladies.' They certainly don't expect to find women in law enforcement. It makes my job easier."

For safety Donna drove her assigned car, an unmarked tan Satellite, to a town 50 miles from Norwood and registered at a motel. By telephone, she arranged a meeting with the informant.

Jimmy, a scruffy man of 30 in bill cap and dirty jeans, convinced Donna he was serious, that he was "under the hammer" and willing to cooperate. But before they made even the first contact, Donna would have to learn all she could about Jimmy—where he lived, what he ate and drank, his girlfriend, his hangouts, his buddies.

"If I get in a tight spot and don't know these things, then the people I'm dealing with might get suspicious," Donna explains.

She spent hours with Jimmy, learning his habits, memorizing his haunts. Then Jimmy took Donna to meet Hugh, a grimy, tatooed man about 40 who operated a drug ring from his tavern.

"You stay up front and get yourself a beer," Jimmy said. "Old Hugh and me have got some talking to do."

Jimmy and Hugh disappeared into a back room. Donna perched on a bar stool and ordered a can of Schlitz. She flipped open the top and poured the beer into a glass herself. When she's undercover she never drinks cocktails or beer on draft. There's always the likelihood that someone has slipped drugs into her drink, a chance she can't afford to take.

Before she took the last sip, Jimmy returned. He had made a deal with Hugh for Donna to buy cocaine. Now her role was established, her first contact made.

Donna continued to visit the tavern with Jimmy, and each time Jimmy made a private deal in the back room. Eventually, she was invited into the back room—alone. This time Jimmy sat at the bar swilling beer while Donna made her own purchase.

"Wanta make some *real* money, Joni?" Hugh pocketed the crumpled bills Donna had just handed him. "You can work for me, you know."

Donna puffed a ball of cigarette smoke at Hugh, watched it rise and expand. "Hell, I don't know nothing 'bout tending bar."

"Tending bar ain't what I had in mind." Hugh smiled knowingly, exposing a row of yellowed teeth. "You can make lots of money working the back room. Ask my wife. She'll tell you what she makes back here."

The back room, Donna says, the same room she was buying drugs in, was used also for prostitution. Donna declined, but she declined delicately. She couldn't afford to hurt Hugh's feelings. She'd need his assistance for a long time.

Donna played the Joni role, winning Hugh as a friend, coaxing him to introduce her to others in the drug business. She spent three days a week in Norwood, working almost around the clock, then returned to Nashville to resume her life and work there for the rest of the week. Gradually, she met more and more unsavory characters until, three months after her first meeting with the tavern owner, Donna decided it was time to "come out." At the raid 15 arrests were made.

"That was an excellent roundup," Donna says. "In street cases, there would have been 30 to 60 arrests. But in the upper echelons of drug dealers, like Hugh and his friends, you get fewer. They're the biggies."

Donna still shudders when she's traveling down an interstate highway and sees the Norwood exit sign. "I guess I always will," she says.

The Norwood case was an extremely dangerous one. At any

18   BREAKTHROUGH: *Women in Law Enforcement*

Donna making a purchase of drugs (simulated; photo by John Gurnee, Jr.)

moment, Jimmy could have decided to squeal or Donna could have overplayed her role and created suspicion. The result is obvious. She'd have been wiped out, the evidence silenced.

Even after the trials, Donna's life was still endangered. From jail, Hugh contacted a hit man to kill Donna. The price he offered was $10,000. A cell mate overheard the arrangements and tipped off the prison guard.

"Some of the agents from the bureau called on Hugh in his cell and explained that his physical well-being could no longer be guaranteed if any harm came to me," Donna says. "Hugh's a pro. He got the message. The contract was rescinded."

The Norwood case was a narrow escape for Donna, but she doesn't dwell on the dangers. Actually, all of her cases are dangerous.

"It's after they're over that it all washes over me," Donna says. "I think back over how it would have been if everything hadn't gone right. Then I try to turn it into something positive. I go over my errors and why I made them. It's so easy to make a mistake. Like slipping into police jargon. We all use it. It's like second nature. For instance, we say 'ten-four' instead of 'okay.' If I were to slip up and use that when I'm undercover it would be disastrous. You really can't relax a minute."

In the Norwood case, Donna had two surveillance agents assigned to her. If she didn't call in regularly they'd go out looking for her. Other times she's wired like an astronaut, with every word she speaks, every breath she breathes picked up at headquarters. But sometimes Donna works with no surveillance at all. "I'm just out there all alone," she says. "It gets scary."

Donna never played cops and robbers when she was growing up in Nashville and never anticipated becoming a law-enforcement officer. In fact, she can't remember a time during her childhood when she didn't dream of becoming a nurse. While her friends played "dress up" and wheeled their dolls in carriages, Donna wore white and pretended to be a nurse. Her hero was Florence Nightingale, and her favorite fictional characters were Cherry Ames and Sue Barton, both nurses. In one book Sue Barton, student nurse, underwent an appendectomy and, while recuperating in the hospital, saved a woman's life.

"That book just set me afire," Donna says. "I prayed I'd have appendicitis and went around punching on my side to see if it was sore. To be in the hospital sounded so glamorous. I just knew I'd save someone's life just like Sue."

Donna's prayer was never answered, her ambition never realized. As a student in the nursing program at Vanderbilt University in Nashville she quickly became disillusioned. A nursing degree, she learned, requires math and chemistry, her two worst subjects. She struggled and made it into the second year. Studying late into the night, Donna began to examine her motives, to question her choice of career. Did she choose nursing because of the glamour of Sue Barton's experience? Or were there other, more valid, reasons?

Eventually, Donna made a self-discovery that turned her thinking around. To her, life was a drama and she longed to play an active role. When she was a child, nursing was one of the few professions open to women that would satisfy that longing. Now there were others. She'd find one.

In high school Donna had taken karate lessons on weekends. Her instructor was Ken, now her husband. At the time, Ken was an engineering student at Vanderbilt, with teaching as a sideline.

Donna was good at karate and earned a green belt. In 1971, while Donna was a sophomore, the two were married. Donna helped Ken with his classes, and the two of them gave demonstrations across the state. The experience was satisfying to Donna and led to another self-discovery. Not only was she consumed with the drama of life but she was deeply concerned with its preservation.

When the city of Nashville secured a federal grant for the development of a rape crisis center, Donna was approached as one of two women to coordinate and run the operation. To Donna this was reason enough to drop out of school. From this position she became a spokesperson for rape defense and gained national recognition as a special guest on the Tom Snyder "Tomorrow" television talk show.

In her new job Donna came in contact with law-enforcement officers for the first time. She liked what she saw. But the officer who impressed her most was a female detective who spoke at one of Donna's conferences on self-defense. Ken, meanwhile, had grown disillusioned with engineering. He, too, admired the law-enforcement officers in his karate classes and was intrigued with their work. When the rape center grant was terminated, both

Donna practicing martial arts

Donna and Ken applied to the Nashville city-county police department (known as Metro Police Department).

At the time there were eight women already employed, all working with juveniles.

"That's typical," Donna says. "Women were always assigned to juveniles or to work with women victims, none of the real police work that men did. But I wanted something else. I wanted a patrol job."

Both Donna and Ken scored high on all the tests and were summoned for interviews, 15 minutes apart. Ken went in first and emerged beaming. He was hired. Then Donna went in for her interview. The chief of police thanked her for applying but explained that he couldn't hire two from the same family.

"But there are two married couples on the force now," Donna countered.

"They were already working here when they got married," the chief replied.

Donna resisted the rationale. To her, a married couple was a married couple. The rule that no married couple could work on the force was already invalid. She had scored as high on the tests as Ken, there were other openings in the department, so why couldn't she, too, have the job?

"He finally offered me a position as typist downstairs," Donna says. "That made me mad. Very, very mad."

She went home, cried, threw a few things. The next day she called an attorney—a woman.

"I just wasn't going to take that lying down. I planned to file suit," she says. "But before I raised a great big stink I thought I'd better be pretty darned sure that law enforcement was what I wanted."

Vanderbilt at the time did not offer a degree in criminal justice or courses in law enforcement. But they did have one thing Donna wanted—an opening for a security guard. Donna applied, was hired and became the first woman to work the foot patrol by night. Uniformed and armed, she trekked across the wide expanse of campus under cover of darkness—and found she did indeed like law enforcement.

"All the while I kept sticking pins at the Metro Police Department, pulling strings, needling, getting to know officers on the force," she says. "I was still on the preferred list and my name had to keep coming up regularly, so I just applied pressure."

Six months later, Donna received a letter from the Metro Park Patrol Division offering her a position. She'd be one of the first two women to patrol municipal parks. It wasn't what she wanted, not what she applied for, but it was a giant step in the right direction. She took it.

"Basically the job was patrol work," Donna says. "I was assigned a squad car and usually patrolled alone. In summer I had a chance to do some undercover work with drug and alcohol violations. I'd wear plain clothes to the beach and picnic areas and just walk around looking. That really sharpened my vision. I got so good I could spot a Budweiser can at 200 paces."

The undercover work put Donna in touch with officers in the Metro vice squad. When they arrested a woman, they'd ask Donna to search her. The officers in turn suggested that Donna be put on special assignment to work on undercover narcotics.

"I knew this was entry level," Donna says. "They were just using me because they'd discovered that undercover women do well in narcotics. I wasn't exactly dazzled by their offer. I thought anyone working in narcotics had to be pretty stupid. To be uniformed and armed is dangerous enough. But to conceal your weapon and deliberately put yourself in jeopardy was unthinkable."

Yet she was ready for a change, a greater challenge. She took the job. For the first few months, Donna worked in the roughest section of Nashville, ferreting out heroin sales. Within a month, she was hooked on the job.

"Just like my boss told me, I found it addictive," she says. "You see a drug nest wiped out, you feel good about yourself, and you want to go for more."

The lure of the job was much more than the blend of excitement and danger, the sweet taste of success. To Donna, the use of drugs and narcotics is the nation's number one problem. She's seen the perils firsthand.

One of Donna's cases involved juvenile sellers and users on the street level. She worked her way into their circles, sitting around in their haunts while they smoked marijuana and drank beer or wine.

"Some of them were junior-high kids and it nearly blew my mind," Donna says. "If they flunked a test they'd go smoke pot. If they got mad or had a problem at home they'd drink wine. That's no solution at all. They're not learning any coping mechanisms. They're just running away. All their lives they'll have their share of failures and disappointments, just like the rest of us. They need to learn how to deal with them."

The undercover work was only part-time, but Donna was good at it and her reputation grew. When the Tennessee Bureau of Investigation approached her with an offer, Donna took less than 30 seconds to say yes. Now her days and nights are spent almost evenly divided between work in the field and work in the office. She averages about three months a year away from home. On her days in the office she checks messages, reads and clips tips and pertinent information from newspapers, and brings her files up to date.

"Practically every day I get calls from some mother who has found marijuana in her son's room and doesn't know what to do about it," Donna says. "The bureau doesn't handle requests like that, but the state has agencies that do. So I put them in touch."

In 1981, Donna and Ken were both awarded a three-month scholarship to the Federal Bureau of Investigation Academy in Quantico, Virginia. There were 242 men in session and six women. Donna and Ken were the first married couple to attend

Donna ready for action (simulated; photo by John Gurnee, Jr.)

Donna posing as a professional business woman (photo by Chip DeVilbiss; make-up by Rick Brown)

simultaneously. They stayed in separate dormitories but saw each other every day and shared the same quarters on weekends. Donna studied for a management level position in law enforcement.

Unlike most law-enforcement officers, Donna doesn't dwell on physical fitness. When she feels it's necessary, she works out on gym equipment.

"But I'm no fitness bug," she says. "Running bores me. Usually the chases are in short spurts, and I can handle that fine."

Nonetheless, she's trim with a glow of health, and she intends to keep it that way. "There's nothing worse than fat officers as far as image is concerned," she says. "But as for fitness, I've spent the last 10 years of my life preparing for conditions that may never come up. I've never been attacked, never had to kick anybody other than at training sessions, never fired a gun other than on the rifle range. But if the situation demands, I'm ready for it."

Donna was a feminist long before the national trend. Although a lifelong resident of Nashville, proclaimed capital for country music, she refuses to listen to the music it produces because it shows women in negative roles and being "put upon." Working as security guard at Vanderbilt, Donna learned that she was making $.25 an hour less than her male counterparts.

"I marched right in and demanded an increase," she says. "Of course, they played dumb and pretended they didn't know about the discrepancy."

Shortly after Donna became a law-enforcement officer she watched Angie Dickinson play the role of Pepper on "Police Woman," a television series. "I saw three shows and wanted to throw something at the set every time," she says. "Pepper always did something stupid and was never able to get out of it by herself. She had to wait for someone to rescue her. Some of the things Pepper did were illegal and would have gotten the case thrown out of court. You just can't do things like that. I'd sit there and think of twelve different ways I could have gotten out of the situation. Or better yet, twelve ways to keep from getting into the mess."

"Hill Street Blues," on the other hand, gives a much truer picture of police work, Donna says.

Like most law-enforcement officers, Donna suffers a sense of isolation. "You see so much that goes on out there," she says. "Then you're with people who know nothing about the street. You try to tell someone about it, and you get a blank stare. They just don't understand what you're talking about, so they change the subject."

Gradually she, like other officers, has narrowed her friends to only those within the same profession except for one or two comrades from school days.

Stress is a constant companion. Before Donna goes on a new case, she often gets diarrhea. And when she comes off a case it takes her a while to unwind. Just after the Christmas incident with Sam, she found her knees so weak she could hardly walk. And she spent the rest of the night riding with Ken on his beat.

"I can spill my guts to Ken, because he knows what it's like out there," Donna explains. "It would be hard on a marriage if your husband doesn't understand. You just can't go home and tell someone about raiding a junkie's house and running into a comatose wife, whose husband is out buying more dope and whose three young kids are drinking sour milk while there's rotten food on the table and excrement all over the floor and nobody's doing a thing about it. Now who would believe all that?"

To relax after such a day Donna reads, does needlepoint, writes articles for law-enforcement journals and manages to approach the next day with the same enthusiasm.

If you're interested in a career in law enforcement, Donna suggests that you begin early. Get involved in Explorer Scouting programs, especially those that deal directly with law enforcement.

Donna and Ken relaxing in their yard

Check out police cadet programs in your area. This puts you in touch with criminal justice at high-school age. If you're still interested, then select a college that offers a degree in criminal justice. Study sociology and math and/or computer science. And take martial arts, not because it's a necessity but because it increases self-confidence.

"Actually, your biggest physical problem as a woman will be fending off the advances of men," Donna warns. "But you can learn to deal with that."

Donna feels the percentage of women in law enforcement will rise rapidly for a few years, then there'll be a leveling off. "At that time, employers will be much more selective, so you'll need more preparation than I had," Donna adds. "The bureau now requires a college degree, although I was hired without one."

Donna has since returned to college part-time and has earned her degree. Now she is eligible to move into management, and she may someday decide to do just that. From a management position she'll be able to actively recruit women—not for the sake of women but for the sake of law enforcement. She knows firsthand their special aptitude for undercover work, their success rate in other areas of this demanding career.

Sometimes when Donna is stuffing her hair under a wig, outlining her eyes in vivid green and planning her strategy for another ominous assignment, she pauses to wonder whether her work is worth the risk and the ridicule. Cops and undercover agents are constantly bombarded with criticism and scorn by a segment of society that views them as bullies and calls them demeaning names like "the fuzz." It's not easy to stomach.

And what about her own safety? Will she again return unscathed to familiar surroundings, see Ken, hear the dogs greet her even before she unlocks her door? Good questions.

Then Donna remembers those junior-high students at their neighborhood hangout, their minds dulled by pot and wine, their futures threatened with crime and violence. Suddenly she knows the answer.

Donna slides a gun into the pocket of her jeans, takes a last critical look at herself in the mirror and heads for the door.

> *"Choice in life is essential. It pleases me to know that women who love the sea and the reef life as I do can now choose to combine that love with a law-enforcement career."*

Jenna Garman Sprecher, Florida Marine Patrol

JENNA SPRECHER WAS BONE-WEARY AS SHE AND OFFICER Mark Walker swung their 26-foot boat around and headed for shore. The luminous dial on Jenna's watch alerted her that it was already past midnight, the knock-off time for their 9-hour shift, yet they were still 45 minutes away from Key West, their home port.

It had been a long night, patrolling the waters off the Florida Keys. The September sky was starless, an angry wind whipped salt spray into their faces, and ocean waves bit at their boat.

"Worst patrol I've had so far," Jenna called above the splash of water, the roar of the motor.

"You'll see worse." Mark cut a path between two 7-foot waves, setting the boat on a smoother course. "Just wait."

Mark should know. He was an old-timer at the job. But it was different with Jenna. She was only two weeks out of Police Minimum Standards School and brand-new as a marine patrol officer for the state of Florida. During these two weeks she had been riding shotgun with senior officers until her probationary period was up. Soon she'd be assigned a boat of her own.

Jenna's heart plumped up with pride when she recalled the circumstances of her hiring. There had been 1,000 other applicants on the roster and 100 interviewed the same week. The competition was keen. But Jenna's record was impressive. Although she was only 24 years old, she had chalked up some credentials that made her an excellent choice for the Marine Patrol. She was certified to teach scuba diving, lifesaving and water safety. She was an instructor in cardiopulmonary resuscitation (CPR). She had passed courses in power boating, studied sociological reasons for drug abuse and had even excelled in underwater photography. All of these assets helped outweigh the one fact that filled Jenna with doubt—the state of Florida had never employed a woman for the Marine Patrol.

But Jenna was prime choice. She was hired in March 1977. And when, three months later, she graduated from the Minimum Standards School for law-enforcement officers, she ranked top in the entire class, the rest of them men. Now she was being watched and she knew it. As the first female officer she had to prove herself, not only for her own sake but also for the benefit of other women who might apply later. As a rookie she was assigned long night shifts, such as the one tonight, but they helped her demonstrate her worth. She liked the challenge.

Jenna dried her salt-sprayed hands on her pants leg and swung her binoculars over the dark expanse of water. There—there on the horizon—a dark form loomed: a boat, moving in short spurts, its lights blinking off and on. Because of its erratic movement, Jenna suspected the boat was involved in trap robbing, a constant menace in Florida waters. Saltwater thieves scurry about under cover of night, lifting lobster traps implanted by commercial fishermen and selling the stolen catches for big money.

To marine patrol officers, a trap robbery is like a convenience store holdup on land, an ongoing problem. Lobster fishermen consider it a direct assault on their livelihood and threaten to kill the robber. The Marine Patrol tries to intervene, to make an arrest instead of having to investigate a murder at sea.

"Starboard at two o'clock," Jenna called in nautical lingo to Mark. "Suspicious maneuvers. We'd better check."

As Mark turned to starboard course, Jenna trained the searchlight on the dark hull. It was a 62-footer, dressed out like an authentic commercial crawfish boat. But lots of trap robbers use standard fishing boats to avert suspicion. When the name of the boat became visible, Jenna radioed the information to headquarters.

Mark meanwhile had his hands full trying to maneuver the boat close in. He made two or three swipes, gaining a little footage, but the waves washed him away again. Finally, he drew within 10 feet.

Jenna flipped the radio system to the loudspeaker setting. "Florida Marine Patrol," she shouted. "Request permission to come aboard to check your papers."

The bow was wet and slippery as an eel. Mark had to give Jenna a hand up. The boat rocked precariously; it was hard to hold her balance. Between the two boats churned the dark, menacing water, slapping at the hulls like angry hands. If she were to fall, her heavy shoes and gun would take her straight down. But Jenna refused to look. When the patrol boat dipped forward she seized the opportunity, grabbed the gunnel of the crawfishing boat, threw her legs over the ridge and dropped aboard. Before her stood two men in faded clothes—one young, one middle-aged. Both appeared to be Cuban and men of the sea.

"Captain, I'd like to see your papers," Jenna said, her voice controlled and businesslike.

"One moment," the young one replied, his Latin accent detectable. "I'll go to the cabin and get them." His jeans disappeared through the doorway.

"What's your name?" Jenna pleasantly asked the remaining man.

"No comprendo." He rolled the "r."

Jenna scanned the deck. The vessel was indeed a crawfishing boat, but it was loaded with wire fish traps, illegal to transport or set in Florida waters. The captain returned, handed Jenna his papers. The federal documentation papers were in order, but registration to fish in Florida waters was missing. Again Jenna asked the captain for his Florida papers.

"We've broken no law," the captain protested. "We've been fishing at sea, not here. Now we're headed for the Cay Sal Banks, and we went into Key West to get ice for the trip."

"Then I'll have to examine your sea catch," Jenna said.

The captain ushered her to an ice box and lifted the lid. The smell of rotten food jumped out like a jack-in-the-box. Putrid eggs, soured milk, lunch meat turned green. "See? No fish," the captain grinned.

To Jenna his grin was false, a cover-up. She wasn't taken in. A fishing excursion to Cay Sal Banks usually lasted two or three days. These men would never start out with rotten food. She slammed the lid on the ice box and headed toward the bow.

"I'd like to verify that you have no catch in your forward hold," she said.

Mark, meanwhile, was circling, trying to stay close to keep the searchlight trained on Jenna and the men. A wave brought him closer. "What's the problem?" he shouted.

"No problem," Jenna called back. "Please illuminate the forward hull. I'm going up to check the front hold."

Suddenly the captain stepped into her path, his arms folded resolutely across his chest.

"You have no search warrant," he snapped.

"No warrant necessary. I'm just checking for your seafood products," Jenna replied. "Anyway, you're already under arrest for being in Florida waters without legal papers and for transporting illegal traps."

Jenna brushed past the captain and tugged at the heavy fish traps atop the hold, getting no help from the men. Mark tried to hold the searchlight steady, but the current had him. The light came and went. Finally, Jenna got the top cleared and was about to lift the lid.

"No use going any farther," the captain said. "We're loaded to the gunnels with marijuana."

"What?" Jenna gasped, her knees suddenly watery, her heart revving up like an outboard motor.

"We're loaded with grass," the captain repeated, his voice small and despairing against the roar of the sea. "It's in the hold."

"Line up against the gunnel and stay in plain view." Jenna unsnapped the handcuffs from her belt, locked them on the four wrists. "If you move, I'll take action."

She flipped up the lid. There, wrapped in burlap, rested the top layer of what later turned out to be 450 bales of prime Colombian marijuana headed for the USA. A major bust.

On Mark's next sweep, Jenna called him the news.

"My God, are you all right?" he gasped, swinging the boat close enough to hand her a shotgun.

Now to get to the mainland with her prisoners and their contraband. Jenna was to pilot the captive vessel and Mark was to ride alongside in the patrol boat. But the ignition sputtered under Jenna's touch, the motor refused to turn over. And Jenna recognized the problem. The smugglers had resorted to an old trick. They had installed a system that only they could operate. It gave them an extra edge over an officer, another chance to seize control. Sometimes it worked. This time it didn't.

Left: Jenna and Officer Daniel Sievers loading up for a patrol
Right: Jenna on water patrol

"You take her in," Jenna removed the handcuffs from the captain. "But no funny stuff. Straight to Key West."

Jenna perched on the bow, her shotgun poised for action, as the two boats sped to shore. Florida Marine Patrol's only female officer had proved herself—handily.

"That's when the other officers slowly began to accept me, to believe I could handle the job," Jenna says. "We later discovered guns in the center cabin of that vessel. If those men had been violent they could have shot me the minute I boarded. Then they could have blown Mark right off his boat. Our bodies would have been lost at sea, and those smugglers would be free."

Even though this was Jenna's first felony arrest, and one that yielded a large contraband, she still has misgivings. If she'd been more experienced, she would have suspected marijuana the moment her feet hit the deck of the offending vessel.

"When you're dealing with grass, you learn to use all your senses," she explains. "I didn't use my nose on that one. If I had known what the raw bailed stuff smelled like, I would have detected it earlier. If that were to happen today, I'd recognize raw grass instantly."

34   BREAKTHROUGH: *Women in Law Enforcement*

Jenna and Major Lavelle Pitts after an 85-foot dive to Gunsmoke, a sunken craft involved in a murder

Jenna regularly confronts the smuggling aspect of her job. About 80 percent of all imported illegal drugs come into this country via Florida. And Key West, where she was stationed at the time, is the choice port. It's the last island in the narrow string of keys off the Florida coast, far removed from heavy population and a difficult area to patrol.

The opportunity to help wipe out drug felonies gives Jenna incentive and motivation. But it's not her main purpose in taking this job. She has a reason much closer to her heart: Jenna is an environmentalist.

In line of duty she's done many things that give her a heady sense of accomplishment and purpose—tracking down smugglers, diving for victims of a drowning, arresting illegal boat handlers. One time she was even involved in a heralded diving operation to retrieve murder evidence from the sunken shrimp boat, *Gunsmoke*, lurking 85 feet deep in shark-infested waters. But her real joy derives from preserving the irreplaceable and threatened gifts of nature.

The Florida Marine Patrol operates as a law-enforcement agency under the Department of Natural Resources. Its major function is to protect Florida's unique wealth—its everglades, coral reefs, mangrove swamps, each with its own breed of wildlife, some of which cannot be found in any other place in the world.

The main difference between marine and land patrol is the type of vehicle employed. Instead of sprinting to a squad car and cruising designated roads, Jenna jumps into a patrol boat. Her beat is a watery expanse that extends nine miles into the Gulf of Mexico, three miles into the Atlantic Ocean. While stationed at Key West, Jenna spent much of her time patrolling the priceless reefs that hug Florida's Atlantic coastline, the only prominent coral reefs on the entire continent.

Florida's reefs are composed of a colony of tiny living organisms called polyps, some no larger than a pinhead. Almost 100 different species decorate the ocean floor in intricate patterns of unspeakable beauty, clustering together like an underwater housing project. Their maze of tiny crevices and crannies form "apartments" for rainbow-hued baby fish, for lobsters, crabs and shellfish, for microscopic organisms and a host of other sea animals. Formed thousands of years ago, the reefs are precious not only as a scenic spot for divers. They provide benefits that even the most landlocked citizen of the United States can enjoy.

36   BREAKTHROUGH: *Women in Law Enforcement*

Jenna on island surveillance

Coral reefs, for instance, are living laboratories where scientists and educators can learn and teach about oceans and their inhabitants. They provide shelter from storms, diverting high-tossing waves that might otherwise wash away a portion of the mainland. And they're actually a "factory" for manufacturing sand. Fish browsing and bumping against the reef produce about two and a half tons of sand per acre every year. Some of the sand washes ashore to form beaches, some of it spreads into a meadow of seagrass where crustaceans and mollusks habitate and some of it is used in the construction of buildings. And who doesn't enjoy the seafood made possible by the protection of coral reefs!

"We're trying to preserve the things we love and need," Jenna says. "It took thousands of years for coral reefs to form. Now they're in real danger."

Their biggest threat, she says, is from people. Tourists and divers pick up small chips of coral because they look so beautiful underwater. The specimens start to smell, the colors fade and portions of the coral reef end up in a trash can in New Jersey or along the side of a road in Kansas. This distresses Jenna. Part of her job is to give public lessons in ecology, in boating safety and marine law. She teaches with verve.

A segment of a coral reef

* * *

Jenna's love of nature is a spin-off from her childhood. Her parents, convinced that Jenna and her brother and sister should spend at least a part of their youth in a rural setting, moved to a farm-ranch in the picturesque countryside near Potomac, Maryland. The move extracted a sacrifice in time and effort on the part of her father, a prominent Washington, D.C., attorney.

"My father literally gave us two extra hours a day," Jenna says. "He had to commute forty miles to downtown Washington, he spent two hours every day en route. But he never complained. It was worth it to him just to see his children grow up away from the city clutter."

One of Jenna's earliest recollections is receiving a Shetland pony, Butchie, on her third birthday. With the pony, she was given responsibility. She had to groom, feed and take care of her new pet. But responsibility wasn't the only thing she learned. Soon she was doing special things, like jumping her pony in horse shows at the age of four. From this she advanced into swimming, riflery, canoeing and archery, activities her peers were not yet involved in. Jenna displayed a special aptitude for learning fast and well, for coordination. She often surpassed her brother, two years her senior, in sports. Yet she was never made to feel more special, or her brother less special.

"My father never made allowances for his daughters," she explains. "We were all treated alike, although our abilities were different. I think his attitude is what has made it possible for me to survive in the male-dominated spheres I've worked in. I didn't think in terms of male jobs or female jobs."

On weekends and long summer days, Jenna and her father went for extended hikes in the woods. They picked their way through briars and brambles, their eyes alert to scurrying squirrels, woodchucks or a sprinting wild rabbit. Her father pointed out birds and leaves and wild flowers. "He respects all life and instilled in us a love for all living creatures," Jenna says. "I became an idealistic conservationist."

In the evenings, Jenna's mother set aside the usual nursery rhymes and Mother Goose stories and told her children an original tale of a family of mice, the Oscar Jasper family. As the Sprecher children grew, so did the young Jasper mice.

Jenna's early childhood was indeed happy. But at age 10,

Jenna underwent a trauma long remembered for its pain. Her family moved to the suburban community of Bethesda, Maryland, closer to her father's office. For the first time in her life, Jenna became conscious of something she was quite unable to change—her height.

She had always been taller than average. But so were her sister and brother, and her parents both measured over 6 feet tall. Today, Jenna stands 6'3" and carries her height with pride. But as a fifth grader, she towered over her new classmates. They pointed and chided and made her days miserable. Suddenly Jenna, despite the democracy she had experienced at home, found she was "different."

"The cruelty of young people amazes me to this day," she says. "To be criticized and ridiculed for something I couldn't help was hard to accept."

But the worst was yet to come. Her largest growth spurt shot her up to a full 6 feet height at age 13. Now she was not only taller than her classmates but she towered over her teachers and the school principal as well.

"It was certainly no fun," Jenna recalls. "I felt ostracized by my own classmates. They didn't include me in their activities, so I just stood around alone most of the time."

But Jenna discovered she could make a choice. She could either suffer in silence, accepting her height as a handicap. Or she could use it as an asset. She chose the latter.

Jenna funnelled her energy into sports. She signed up for basketball, for tennis and volleyball. She practiced after school, her mind concentrated on becoming a better player, perfecting her game. Her athletic prowess carried her through high school. Every team wanted her. She was captain of the girls' basketball and field hockey teams. She won honors in track and field. She was a winner on the area swim team. And in her senior year, Jenna served as special assistant to the physical education department, helping girls with problems in sports.

Her summers were spent studying about animals, spurred by the prospect of becoming a doctor of veterinary medicine when she grew up. But an event during Jenna's teens dramatically changed her ambition. With her family, she vacationed in the Virgin Islands, where she was introduced to a creation of nature compelling enough to turn her life around—the coral reef.

"Seeing the reef for the first time was one of the most profound experiences of my entire life," Jenna says. "I felt forever bound to the sea."

Without consciously realizing it, Jenna began at that moment to prepare herself for a career that would indeed bind her to the sea. She took lessons in snorkeling, then later in scuba diving. Exploring the newfound underwater wonders, she thrilled to the brilliance of the skittering fish, the verdure of ocean vegetation, the rich textures of coral.

How futile it now seemed to worry about her height. The pain of a faraway loneliness seemed to drop away as Jenna felt herself grow in her own sense of self-worth. She was learning new skills, making new friends. This time the skills were ones she chose because she liked them, not just to fill empty hours after school.

When Jenna returned home from that first trip to the Virgin Islands, she signed up for all the biology courses her school offered. Marine biology remained her passion, and she lived for the two weeks each year when her family would again visit the Caribbean. Each year, they chose a different island, and each year Jenna probed the island until she felt as familiar to the mangroves as a sea lizard, as native to the beach as a sand crab. She studied local cultures, talked with strangers, always storing away information she'd use when she, too, lived by the sea.

In the fall of 1970, Jenna migrated south to begin her college education at a school that seemed to be designed just for her—the University of Miami at Coral Gables, Florida, near the ocean and the reefs. Her major was anthropology, with emphasis on marine archaeology. Her minor was graphic art. The two subjects blended like sea and sand years later when Jenna was selected for special summer field studies of pre-Columbian wrecks at Port Royal, Roatán. Not only could she dive to find and examine the sunken remains but she could sketch and graph them. For preparation, she took an intense 100-hour research diver course at Miami's Rosentheil School of Marine and Atmospheric Sciences.

Jenna's college years became a breathless blend of studies and athletics. When her sister signed up for prelaw courses, Jenna added a job to her already tight schedule so she could help her parents financially. Because she attended classes from 9:00 A.M. until 1:00 P.M., then studied until the supper hour, a night job seemed the solution. But where? The answer, it turned out, nudged Jenna another step toward her present career. She signed on as the first woman security guard for the university, patrolling the wide expanse of campus by foot and auto from midnight until 8:00 A.M. This only left one hour for changing clothes, grabbing breakfast and dashing to class. And only a few hours to sleep between supper and the midnight shift.

Jenna had held other jobs during summers, mostly singing and playing her guitar at coffeehouses back home. But her new job captured her interest. She found, much to her surprise, that she enjoyed law enforcement.

On her days off, she and her fiancé, Steve Solly, a talented Miami welder 10 years her senior, would head for the keys to dive near the coral reefs.

Jenna's education was interrupted twice. The first time occurred when her father became ill with cancer. Jenna was devastated not only by her father's vulnerability but by the realization that he wouldn't live forever, a fact she had never confronted. She returned home. Although he suffered the loss of an eye during the ensuing months, her father regained his health and was soon active again.

Jenna resumed her studies in Coral Gables but stopped short of graduation. In June 1976, she and Steve, who had been patient and supportive during her years of upset schedules and delayed schooling, were married. The Young Men's Christian Association (YMCA) in Miami offered Jenna a job as scuba-diving instructor in Key West, an opportunity she found almost irresistible.

Key West is the southernmost city in the continental United States, the last island in the Florida Keys. With rocky shores, sandy beaches and weathered homes, the island's charm and casual lifestyle have lured a number of famous people to live within its boundaries—Ernest Hemingway, John James Audubon, Tennessee Williams. Its harbor is dotted with an array of seagoing vessels, from the smallest fishing boat to spacious yachts. And its sunset is touted as being among the most beautiful in the world.

But even more appealing was the lure of Jenna's beloved coral reefs, so close to Key West that their dark green shadow could be seen from the shore!

Steve, too, was ready for a change. In Key West, he could contract his welding skills and become his own boss. So in the summer of 1976, the Sollys set out for their new home.

For a while all went well. Jenna's job was to teach a diving safety program to the U.S. Army Corps of Engineers. The Corps had lost an alarming number of men in diving accidents and had contracted with the YMCA for intense training. Jenna, again the only woman in her work surroundings, taught groups consisting of 30 to 40 men. She lectured on physiology, oxygen toxicity, barotrauma and nitrogen narcosis, subjects she had studied for her own certification in lifesaving and water-safety instructing. Then she taught open water sessions in scuba diving and surface air-supply techniques.

The course lasted four weeks, then the center was inactive for a few months. Jenna spent these months earning a small income as a free-lance artist and scuba-diving instructor. She and Steve were trying to build a small nest egg so Jenna could return to Coral Gables for a semester to complete her college degree. But the nest egg was slow to hatch, and Jenna was growing doubtful. She needed a full-time job.

Jenna first learned of the Florida Marine Patrol through one of its members who was teaching marine-related first aid at the YMCA. He was impressed with Jenna's qualifications and experience. He encouraged her to apply but cautioned her that the Marine Patrol had never before hired a woman, a fact Jenna found challenging rather than discouraging.

She and Steve weighed the decision carefully. They discussed the long hours, the rotating shifts, their days and nights of separation. They talked of the dangers Jenna would face, the hours of anxious waiting Steve was sure to experience.

"We knew it was no Sunday afternoon job cruising around on a boat," Jenna says. "In lots of ways, it's more dangerous than land patrol. You're vulnerable out there. You don't have a backup around the corner. It's especially dangerous at night, and we knew I'd be doing a lot of night patrols."

There were other prospects to consider. Jenna would be confronting some hard-core deep-sea fishermen who'd resent a woman with authority in their waters. They'd put her to the test, and she'd have to prove herself time and time again. And many of the men fish at sea in the nude. Would this embarrass her? Or impede her work?

In the end, both Jenna and Steve decided the career was right for her. In May 1977, Jenna signed on with the Florida Marine

Patrol. She has never regretted the decision, although it precipitated a painful period in her life. Her career progressed, but her personal life suffered. Through what she calls a "spiralling loss of friendship and rapport" her marriage was shattered, and Steve returned to Miami.

A keen sense of humor has helped Jenna through some rough spots. Like dealing with the jealousy of some of the patrolmen's wives when they learned Jenna would be riding with their husbands. Or the time when she and Chico, another officer, both of them off-duty, trapped a pair of runaway smugglers in a maze of one-way streets—unarmed! And especially the time when she, single-handedly, boarded a Texas-based shrimp boat in the Keys and discovered a haul of undersized shrimp in the cold-storage bin.

"That captain didn't like one whit being arrested by a woman," Jenna recalls. "To make matters worse, the ship's crew stood on the sidelines sniggering and poking fun at the skipper, who was, incidentally, two inches taller than I and weighed about three hundred pounds."

A patrol officer doesn't pull a gun unless he or she is threatened with a gun or a knife or crowbar. The captain knew this. He wanted to fight it out, then steal away with his catch and head for the Texas shore. Jenna realized she was outsized—and outnumbered if the crew joined the fight. She'd have to use her ingenuity. She called the skipper aside, away from the joking crew.

"Skipper," she said, "we can either do this the easy way or the hard way. The odds are ninety-nine to one that you'll whip me if we have to fight. But there's one chance in a hundred I'll beat your fanny. And just imagine what all the other fishermen will be saying from here to Texas."

The captain scratched his sun-bleached beard, his gaze fixed on the weathered floor of the shrimp boat. Jenna had touched a nerve. No self-respecting skipper could abide the ridicule of being beaten by a woman. To be arrested peacefully was the better choice. He succumbed.

When Jenna reports to work, she wears a gray uniform, black patent man-type shoes, a billed cap, a gun belt equipped with handcuffs, a .357 magnum revolver and bullet pouches with enough ammunition to reload twice. She tucks her long gold-

Jenna working with her macrame

flecked hair under her cap and smooths a film of sunscreen on her nose and lips. Sunburn is a constant threat even in winter, when the chill factor in a moving boat can plummet to 15 degrees Fahrenheit. Aboard the boat, a 21-foot inboard-outboard Continental, she sets her cooler with sandwiches and cold drinks in the console, secures her shotgun inside a chest and slips into deck shoes with rubberized soles so she can maneuver on wet floors.

Then, except for one more chore, she's ready to set out on her 8-hour patrol. While the motor idles, she checks the back of the boat to be sure her bathroom facility (a small enamel potty!) is aboard. There are no flushing commodes on an open boat, and Jenna's only privacy comes from carefully choosing an isolated cove or a spot at sea where no other boats are in view.

Jenna stands at the wheel as she skillfully operates her boat, even though the constant stance tires her back and makes her legs ache. Standing gives her a wider view.

If the water is rough on the bay side and her boat would be endangered, Jenna may zoom out to the ocean. If the bay is teeming with activity, she may elect to patrol that area. In a matter of minutes after leaving the shore, she may pull up beside a pleasure craft and politely hand the captain a citation. "You have divers overboard without displaying your diver's flag," she says. "I'm giving you a citation today. Next time I'll have to take you in." As the captain hoists his diver's flag, Jenna radios headquarters to report the citation. With a smile and a "Good day, sir," she's off to other waters and other duties.

On her next shift, she may drive by auto to the dolphin-training school farther up the Keys to be sure it's being run to specification. Another day, she may dive for bodies or check an oil spill. Next week, she may appear in court to testify on an arrest she made.

Every day is different, every day a test of Jenna's multifaceted abilities. But Jenna's emphasis is always on enforcing the laws created to preserve marine resources. The laws are many and range from protecting endangered species to preventing the dumping of harmful wastes into the sea. And a major part of her job is lecturing the public on safety and conservation.

She paints and plays guitar in her spare time. She runs two miles daily and swims to keep physically fit. It's a life she loves, full of challenge, variety and contact with nature.

Is marine patrol a job she'd recommend for other women?

A broken underwater lobster trap

"Yes," Jenna says, "if she likes being on the water, dealing with people and preserving law and order. But there are certain things she should understand. She can't drink in public, and she shouldn't call attention to herself. And she can't be friends with bohemian types. Sometimes I feel cut off from interesting people because friendship with certain types can destroy the image of a law-enforcement officer. It's hard not to resent that."

Jenna is popular. Wherever she goes, she's greeted by name and teased a little. "Hey, here comes the fuzz," they call as she enters a restaurant or social gathering. But Jenna is hard to overlook. With her height and radiant good looks, she's sure to be noticed. She deals with this by dressing sedately when she's off duty, by keeping her voice low and by carefully choosing the places she frequents.

"But a candidate should understand she'll suffer a loss of privacy and some personal freedom," she explains.

Although only a high school diploma is required, Jenna feels a prospective officer should have two to four years of college. "But not necessarily courses in criminology," she adds. "Any of the social sciences would be excellent backgrounds. But she should definitely take courses in charting and plotting and in

Jenna performing maintenance on her car

boat handling. They look great on your resumé. The courses are offered free by the U.S. Power Squadron and the U.S. Coast Guard Auxiliary, and they're excellent.''

And a candidate must have physical stamina. "In this job you've got to pull crawfish traps when you find an illegal trotline. Those traps weigh seventy-five pounds. You've got to put a boat on a trailer, and you've got to crank the boat by hand. And another thing, you can't mind getting greasy and dirty.''

One job requirement is that all officers must keep their car and boat and trailer in tip-top shape. "That means you must wash, wax, change spark plugs, do tune-ups, change oil and filters. You have to keep rust off the trailer, the boat scrubbed and clean, neatly painted and the engine in working order. You learn these things on the job, and you do most of it during working hours,'' she says.

48   BREAKTHROUGH: *Women in Law Enforcement*

Jenna has recently put into play another trait necessary for her job—adaptability. Like coastal weather, changes in a career such as hers can be rapid and unpredictable. In July 1981, Jenna was promoted to a management position and transferred to Tampa. Now she's in charge of Training and Education for one fourth of the state. The position involves a great deal of traveling while teaching both Marine Patrol officers and the public. Again, Jenna is the only woman. The other three Training and Education officers are men.

Shortly after she moved to Tampa, Jenna met Captain Gabriel Venero of the Tampa Police Department. In December, they were married in what proved to be a lucky blend of similar careers and off-duty interests.

Jenna's new territory sweeps beyond the Everglades to the place where the Gulf of Mexico merges with the Atlantic Ocean. From her new home on the Gulf coast, she can no longer daily view the shadow of her beloved coral reef. But Jenna finds she is furthering the cause of preservation even more in her new job by stressing its importance to the officers in her district and by expanding public awareness through lectures and studies.

The call of the coral is still with her.

"It's amazing to me how cruelly human beings can treat one another for whatever reasons—passion, brutality, greed. I'm glad I have an opportunity to do something about it, or at least to try."

Maureen Anne Higgins, FBI Agent

MAUREEN LAYS THE LETTER ON A CORNER OF HER DESK, removes a knife from the pocket of her white smock and carefully slits the wrapping from the square brown box.

Ordinarily, she would don protective gloves before lifting the lid. But today Maureen already knows, from reading the letter, that the evidence inside the box is intact, that there are no latent fingerprints she could destroy or distort.

Maureen knows other things from reading the letter, facts that pique her curiosity and make her hands anxious to get on with the job. The postmark, for instance. Butte, Montana, far enough across the country to seem like a different world from Maureen's office in the Federal Bureau of Investigation (FBI) building in the nation's capital.

And the crime. A stabbing murder on an Indian reservation. Tangible evidence lurks inside the box. The clothing worn by the suspect and the victim—jeans, T-shirts, socks and boots. They're wrapped in clear plastic, but they still bear the smell of life—the odor of cigarette smoke, of Montana soil, of human sweat. Some of the garments show splotches of a red-brown stain. Two knives are enclosed, supposedly the knives that slashed wounds deep enough to end a life. And jagged shards of glass from broken pop bottles.

Maureen's assignment, handed to her by her unit chief, is to make a blood analysis and to determine what other examinations could be important to the case—such as an analysis of the glass, soil, metal, fabric, fingerprints, hair or fiber. She is instantly alert and extremely cautious as she lifts the lid and fingers the objects. A trace evidence, such as a strand of hair or a delicate fiber, could easily be lost if not handled with the greatest of care. The work is tedious, the results weighty. For Maureen is a forensic scientist. The information she develops could be pertinent to a murder trial.

She rushes the box and its contents to an adjacent laboratory, the Microscopic Analysis Unit, where each piece of evidence is hung over a sheet of plain brown paper and scraped. All unattached particles are gathered from the paper and placed in a pill box. Then the examiners snip a piece of each garment to run more intricate checks for fiber content.

Maureen takes the box, along with the new trace evidence in the pill box, to the Minerology Unit. There the examiners will determine if there are any glass particles present, comparing any samples they find with the shards of glass from the pop bottle. Then Maureen proceeds to the Hair and Fiber Unit, where the examiners will scrutinize the evidence under microscope and compare it with known hair and fiber samples from the victim and the suspect.

While these tests are in progress, Maureen returns to her glass-encased office to face other brown boxes of evidence. They come to her in all sizes, some as small as a jewelry box, others as large as a school locker. But even the smallest can be vital. A rubber cap on the tip of a crutch once served to link a suspect to a brutal murder. And glass particles imbedded in a broom handle once proved that a window pane had been broken from the inside rather than by an alleged intruder. Nothing can be overlooked, nothing tossed away.

Ten days later, the Butte box is returned to Maureen's desk, complete with reports of the lab analyses. The reports excite her. The glass examiner discovered a particle on the sole of one boot. It matches the glass in the pop bottle. But even more convincing is the strand of human hair attached to the suspect's T-shirt. It matches the sample taken from the murder victim at autopsy.

Her interest mounting, Maureen sets aside her other assignments and moves into the serology tests (the examination of liquid blood samples and dried blood stains), which she herself performs. Visually she checks the stain on a T-shirt, on the leg of a jean. To her naked eye, both stains bear the appearance of blood. But she must make certain. She applies chemicals. Now the stains react like blood.

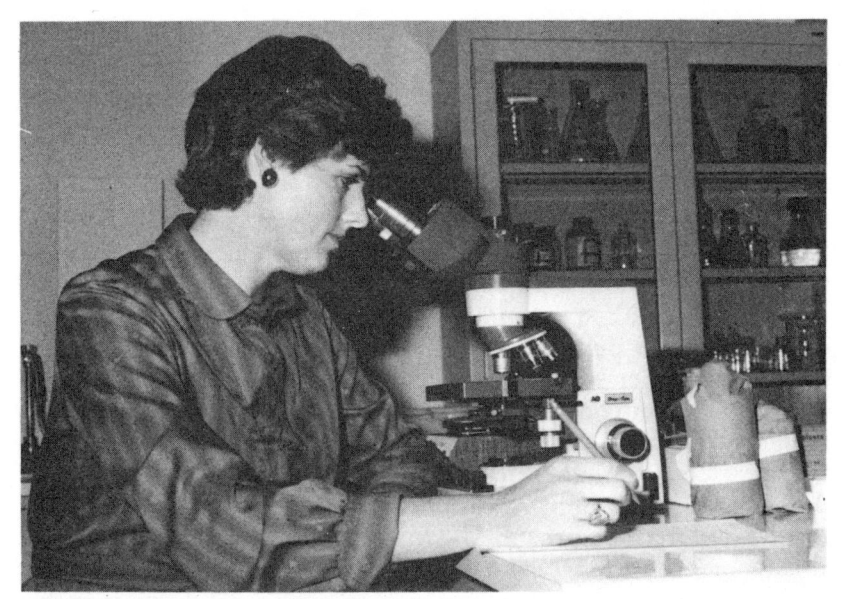

Maureen at her microscope

Maureen moves quickly into the second phase of testing. She removes a small portion of the stained fabric, attaches it to a slide, adds a chemical agent and examines the specimen under a microscope. Red crystals, elongated and shiny, develop as she watches, and Maureen's pulse quickens. Now for the first time she is dealing with a certainty—the presence of blood.

But is the blood human or that of an animal? Snipping a piece of fabric, Maureen extracts the blood in a saline (salt and water) solution and watches the results. It is now certain that the blood contains human protein.

Now Maureen types the blood and finds it to be Type AB. She isolates the six human enzymes, sorts them into types. These enzyme types show up in certain frequencies in the human body and are genetically determined, such as blue eyes or skin color. Although the enzyme tests cannot alone prove or disprove a suspect's innocence or guilt, when considered with other clues, they can become a persuasive factor in court.

Four days later, Maureen completes her tests and writes her report. The report and the sealed box of evidence are returned to the FBI office in Butte.

But her work on the Butte case is not finished. Nine months

after she completes the lab work, Maureen boards an airplane for Montana. For the next three days she appears in court where the murder trial is already in progress. This time she wears no smock. She's dressed in a tailored gray flannel suit, her white blouse tied in a bow at the neck. Maureen is there for one reason—to give the jury an accurate description of how her test results were gleaned. Each juror's attention must be focused on facts rather than on Maureen. That's why she plays down her natural beauty, eliminating flashy colors and gimicky styles.

On the witness stand Maureen testifies as to her findings. The defense attorney peppers her with questions, twists her testimony, tries to addle her so she'll make false statements. Even scientific facts can be misconstrued and made misleading. But Maureen remains calm. She pauses when she needs to, listens carefully to the questions, thinks before she answers.

When her testimony is completed, long before the trial is concluded, Maureen returns to Washington to resume the tests she's already begun on other evidence. Next week she may be in Hawaii testifying in another court of law. In six months she may be stationed in Topeka, Kansas, or Bangor, Maine, as a field investigator, routing out bank robbers or tracking down kidnappers. But today Maureen is a scientist, an examiner of physical evidence, a position she holds because of her background in biology.

"Yet when I'm examining that evidence on my desk I'm no longer a biologist," Maureen says. "I'm a law-enforcement officer dealing with crime. That's what's foremost in my mind."

There's a saying at the FBI that "once an agent, always an agent." Every agent takes the same tests, attends the same academy, undergoes the same training. Each agent is sent into the field to do whatever criminal work is necessary—surveillance, search, arrests, chases. And each agent is subject to be transferred regularly to other locales.

But because some agents have special aptitudes, they are often summoned to Washington for specific assignments. An agent gifted in writing may serve in public relations. One with computer know-how may specialize in extortion cases. In Maureen's case, she holds a Master of Science degree in biology, so her ability in the laboratory is valuable. After serving three years in the field, she was called to Washington, where she is now in her sixth year. Without further training, she could become a gun-toting criminal investigator in any of the 50 states. She's ready to make the move whenever the FBI decides to reassign her.

Maureen's introduction to law enforcement was so natural and gradual as to be almost innate. Her father was a plainclothes detective for the Washington police force. Maureen remembers well his long and erratic hours, the worried look on her mother's face when he was on dangerous assignments, the way the dinner conversation carefully avoided the mention of strategic cases.

Maureen also remembers other occasions when her father's coworkers gathered at the Higgins house for a party. They swapped stories of cases they had worked on in the past—some with happy endings, some tragic, some humorous. Maureen and her brother, three years her junior, listened with enchantment to their tales of a world far removed from their comfortable home.

"They'd repeat the same stories every time," Maureen says with laughter in her brown eyes. "I knew exactly what they'd say next. But I was enthralled. I loved to hear those stories over and over again."

Despite her enchantment with her father's profession, Maureen does not recall ever consciously deciding to become a law-enforcement officer when she grew up. During her childhood she read a lot, exploring a variety of subjects. "Thinking back on it, I sound a bit dull," she smiles and runs a pencil through her light brown curls. "I seemed always to have had my nose in a book."

By the time she reached high school, Maureen had already discovered her favorite field of study—anything in the sciences. Those were the subjects that whetted her curiosity, made her look forward to the next class. But she wasn't sure which science was her favorite until the day she dissected frogs and earthworms in biology class. On that day she realized that biology felt "good" to her, as comfortable as a pair of faded sneakers.

At St. Joseph's College in Emmittsburg, Maryland, Maureen pursued her interest in science, graduating with a Bachelor of Science degree in biology in 1966. "Even with a degree I felt I needed more schooling," she says. "I still wasn't quite ready for the job market. I wanted more specialized training."

So she entered graduate school at Duquesne University in Pittsburgh, Pennsylvania. While studying she worked part-time in the medical research laboratory at a local hospital, gaining a wealth of information both in dealing with biology and with people. Three years later, at the age of 24, Maureen was awarded her graduate degree in biology.

She continued her work at the hospital, now working full time. Her lab work was executed for one reason—for the preservation of life. Now at the FBI lab Maureen deals with specimens of those who choose to eliminate life or of a victim whose life has been eliminated. To Maureen, there's an interesting correlation between the two positions. But each deals with the same two facts of existence—life and death.

While a career in medical research fascinated Maureen, she still yearned to relate more directly to people rather than samples of tissue and blood. With a keen eye on the job market, she hoped to someday find a career that encompassed both. She did.

The year was 1973. Only one year earlier, the FBI had opened its ranks to include women agents. Until then the bureau, which operates under the Department of Justice and deals in kidnapping, extortion, bank robbery, fugitive arrests and the interstate transportation of stolen property, had maintained a stringent profile for its agents. The rules covered race, sex, education and style. Briefly, the agent was a white male with a degree in either law or accounting, trim in size, clad in a conservative suit and tie with white shirt, his hair short and neat. Further, he was required to wear a hat on the street.

When the first two female agents reported for training at the FBI Academy on July 17, 1972, they ushered in a whole new era for both men and women of all races. Now the requirements state that an applicant must simply be a citizen of the United States between the ages of 23 and 35 and hold a degree in law, accounting, language, science, or have four years of college plus three years' work experience. Male agents now can wear colored shirts, add inches to their hair, and pack away their hats in moth balls. For women, the dress code is standard business attire.

Maureen greeted the news with elation. At 28 she was midway in the age bracket. Her education and experience made her particularly attractive. And a jump from medical research to law enforcement was not the quantum leap it might have been for others. Through her father she already knew a great deal about criminal justice. To her it seemed a natural step.

Maureen applied, took a battery of computerized tests, was

called back for interviews (also computerized) and passed the physical examinations. She was accepted for training. "My family took it in stride," she recalls, "but my father was so proud you could almost see his chest puff up. He said it was not only an excellent career choice but an opportunity to do something extremely worthwhile."

Some of her peers chided her, but Maureen was unflappable. She reminded them that she was an FBI agent who, on the face of the application, just happened to be a woman. Exhilarated and happy, Maureen checked into her room at the FBI Academy at Quantico, Virginia, for 15 weeks of concentrated training. There were only four women in a class of 28 men. Each woman was expected to maintain the same academic level as the men, accomplish the same degree of proficiency on the firing range and, except for a modification in the grading of "pull-ups," perform the same exacting physical tasks.

How different Maureen's life suddenly became. Instead of adjusting microscopes, she was handling firearms. Instead of preparing laboratory specimens, she was making simulated arrests. Rather than rushing from lab to lab, she was running two miles a day and doing 50 sit-ups. In class she was studying the elements of

Maureen on the firing range

189 criminal violations, the principles and history of law, and decisions made by the Supreme Court. She learned the techniques of fingerprinting, how to make arrests, searches and seizures, how the field offices are set up. The contrast was challenging. The weeks sped by.

After graduation Maureen was sent to Milwaukee, Wisconsin, for her first assignment. It proved to be a first for the state of Wisconsin, also, for Maureen was the first female FBI agent to work within its boundaries. She was greeted with a flourish from the press, which quoted Maureen's boss as "welcoming her with open arms," then jokingly adding, "no, we'll greet her with a firm handshake."

Her coworkers watched with interest, but Maureen had lots of opportunities to prove herself. Almost at once she was thrust into a plight that merited national attention, a case involving the ingredients of a James Bond movie—a fugitive from justice, robbery, homicide, assault, hostages and a kidnapping.

A seasoned criminal, wanted in a jewelry store holdup, had killed two police officers in Chicago, Illinois, and fled the state. The FBI traced the suspect to Milwaukee, where, on an eventful Thursday afternoon in March 1974, the scenario proceeded like this:

2:30 P.M.—A male FBI agent is shot in an attempt to arrest the suspect at an apartment building in Milwaukee's east side. Suspect flees on foot.

2:45 P.M.—Suspect arrives at the home of a prominent attorney, seizes two children as hostages.

3:10 P.M.—Police and FBI agents surround the house. Suspect demands a getaway car.

3:20 P.M.—Suspect dashes from house holding one child as hostage. As suspect nears the getaway car, child gets free. Suspect is shot.

3:41 P.M.—Suspect is dead on arrival at county hospital.

Maureen's role in this drama, which terminated a 13-year crime spree, is written between the lines. She and her team staked out a 10-block area, stopping all traffic and clearing the streets of pedestrians. Cautiously they patrolled back and forth, monitoring their car radio to keep abreast of the action. If the suspect had made it to the getaway car, Maureen would have been part of the chase. She was armed and alert, ready for whatever role became

Maureen poses with the loot from the Purolator heist.

her lot. She was part of the team. With the FBI, it's teamwork that counts most.

One year later, Maureen was transferred to the Chicago office and was again thrust into dramatic action. With an axe, she hacked at fresh cement in the basement of a home and uncovered sacks of money stolen from Purolator Security in the nation's largest cash heist to date (total $4.3 million).

And the next year, Maureen was part of a task force in a massive raid that wiped out a powerful gambling ring in Davenport, Iowa.

In the latter two cases, Maureen's name and photo appeared in local newspapers, and she was publicly commended. But this isn't the usual chain of events. Normally, FBI agents prefer no public identification. It's safer, it makes their work easier and they have no desire to become public heroes.

Nor do these cases reflect the eight-hour stretches of surveillance, the tedious tracking of clues that may eventually lead nowhere, the mounds of paperwork Maureen must process. "It's not the glamour job you'd expect from watching television shows about big-city cops or movies about small-town sheriffs," she says. "Most of the time our jobs are pretty clear-cut."

Nor does Maureen dwell on the inherent dangers. They are present, of course. But the FBI, like all law-enforcement agencies, takes considerable care to protect its agents. "We don't just dash out without cover and backup," Maureen explains. "Except in cases of extreme emergencies, we plan ahead to avoid such things."

Maureen has never fired a shot in line of duty except on the practice range. This is not unusual. FBI agents fire only in self-defense or in the defense of another human life. The average gun fight lasts only two and a half seconds at an average range of less than 21 feet.

Yet to deal with crime is to deal with the seamy side of life. Most lawbreakers are either angry, unhappy, maladjusted, uncaring or hostile individuals. Coping with these attitudes adds stress to an agent's job. But Maureen, because she is of a scientific bent, handles stress in a manner not everyone could manage.

"I ignore it," she says. "Eventually it goes away. I've given up

Paperwork plays a large role in an agent's job.

worrying about things. I try to meet my schedules the best I can. If someone can't accept a no, I'm sorry but that's the way it is. And I make a point of leaving all the stress behind me when I go home.''

Technically, Maureen is "on call" around the clock. When she's working on a critical piece of evidence in the laboratory, she telephones her office regularly for developments when she's off duty. Once every two months she must spend a weekend officially on call, always within telephone contact.

Maureen, who is 5'10'' tall and weighs 155 pounds, is single and lives in a three-story town house in northern Virginia, about 20 miles from the FBI headquarters. She carpools to work, arriving before 7:30 A.M. and working about 10 to 12 hours daily. This

Maureen in her kitchen

leaves her little time for other pursuits during the week. On weekends, she often makes a laboratory of her kitchen or backyard grill, preparing new recipes to serve her friends. And on Saturdays she'll jump into jeans, pull out her ladder, paint brushes and wallpaper, and redecorate a room from ceiling to floor. "As for going out on the town, I'm always interested in new plays at the Kennedy Center or new restaurants in Georgetown," Maureen says.

After six years in the lab, Maureen looks forward to returning to a field assignment, possibly in a supervisory position. When the call comes, she can leave with little difficulty. She will not be required to return to the academy for a refresher course or undergo rigorous physical training. She stays in good shape with aerobic dancing, by working out in the gymnasium at the FBI building and by taking at least one long skiing trip every winter. Last year it was to Austria.

As for women agents with the FBI, Maureen feels they have proved themselves by professional performance. "Old-timers at the bureau at first didn't approve of female agents," she says. "But now they've seen that we underwent the same training and

Maureen working in her yard

don't expect special treatment. There's really no problem for a woman here unless it's a personal problem she'd have anyplace."

Women excel at surveillance, Maureen notes. "Seasoned criminals can spot a surveillance agent without much trouble," she explains. "But a woman alone, or two females, can go into a restaurant any hour of the day while watching someone, and no one will suspect. Or a man and a woman can sit in a cocktail lounge and observe for an hour or two without arousing suspicion."

Maureen feels that a woman interested in becoming an FBI agent should follow her own inclinations. If she has a specialty, such as language or a science, she should pursue it. Otherwise she should get her college degree, her three-year work experience, then apply. There are 7,800 FBI agents in the country; 370 are women.

"But one word of caution," Maureen adds. "Before she applies, she should be sure she can work pleasantly with people, be a member of the team even under stress, yet be able to demonstrate initiative and independence. That's very important for an agent."

The FBI has developed some startling statistics regarding crime in the United States; there is a murder committed every 24 minutes, a rape every seven minutes, a burglary every 10 seconds. More than 600,000 pieces of evidence enter the lab for analysis every year, creating monumental backlogs for Maureen and the other examiners.

Maureen is appalled at the volume and intensity of crime, of mankind's inhumanity. She has no easy answers, no quick remedies, no formulas for curtailing or preventing such heinous acts. But she does have a commitment that more than overrides the long, tedious hours of work and the dangers she must face. Whether squinting into a microscope or packing a pistol into her pocket, Maureen is poised for the challenge.

She's sitting on ready.

Pepper and her mount

"I feel I have a commitment to make the world a better place to live in. It may sound ridiculous to think I can do this, but I'll certainly give it a try."

Priscilla Pepper Karansky, Mounted Police

PEPPER (IT'S HER REAL NAME) STOPPED, PLOPPED THE CANvas bag on the sidewalk and took a deep breath. The bag was heavy for a 10-year-old. It looked like a fat green pig, its sides bulging with pajamas and slippers, records and books. The sight of it filled Pepper with pleasant memories of the night before, a night spent at her girl friend's house. They stayed up past midnight, talking, reading, even dancing to rock records.

Now it was almost noon, and the bright Arizona sun was growing hotter by the minute. Before her stretched another 12 blocks before she'd reach home, and the blocks in that section of Phoenix were long. She picked up her bag at the very moment a tan-and-white automobile glided to a stop and a police officer alighted.

"Good morning, young lady." He tipped his billed cap, neat and tan like the car. "You headed someplace special?"

"Yes, sir. I mean no, sir." Pepper felt her face grow warm and as pink as an Arizona sunset. "I mean I guess so."

The officer stooped so his face would be on a level with Pepper's. "You know something? It's not so great being out there in the world alone," he said pleasantly. "What's the matter? You having trouble at home or something?"

"Trouble? I don't know what you . . . I'm just . . ." Pepper's words erupted into a giggle. "You must think I'm running away!"

"You mean you're not?" He sounded relieved but not quite convinced. "In that case, why don't you just hop in this nice car and I'll save you a walk." The officer drove her home and escorted her to the door. It was Pepper's first encounter with a law-enforcement officer. She found him nice and kind, even if a bit meddlesome, and she was glad for the ride home.

Her second encounter was of a different nature, years later when she was handed a traffic ticket for making an illegal U-turn in San Diego, California. During the years that separated these two incidents, Pepper hardly gave law enforcement a thought. Certainly she never guessed she would one day become an officer herself.

Nor did she suspect she would gain the distinction of being one of the federal government's first two female mounted officers. However, a Christmas gift the same year Pepper was driven home by the Phoenix police officer may have served as a tip-off had she been engaged in predicting her future.

The gift that Christmas was a horse, a blend of Indian pony and quarter horse purchased by Pepper's parents for $150. Pepper and her two sisters and two brothers were to share the gift.

"I loved that horse so much that the next Christmas my brothers and sisters gave it to me for my own," Pepper recalls. "I petted and groomed Bay Lady, taught her to jump, rode her in the rodeo parade every year. She was my best friend."

Pepper patrolling the beach

Now, as a mounted officer at Golden Gate National Recreation Area near San Francisco, California, Pepper spends more time with a horse than with any other living creature. Five days a week she grooms her mount, then for the next six hours she patrols the beaches, combs the cliffs and woodlands, searches the parks. Her favorite beat is the coastline with its spread of sand dunes, the wind to her face, the taste of salt on her lips. "It makes me feel like Lawrence of Arabia." Pepper lifts her shoulders and breathes deeply. ". . . the way he must have felt on his horse."

To Pepper, the horse is the most beautiful creature alive. But she feels that horses play dumb and don't live up to their potential. "They sold out for food and shelter long ago," she contends. "They're paranoid, and they hallucinate. You can never outguess them. One minute they may dash up a cliff; the next they'll fall asleep beside a rock concert. I've learned to treat them exactly like what they are—a 1,200-pound three-year-old!"

Pepper deals with hundreds of people every day, wears a pistol and stays in radio contact with headquarters. But she considers the horse she's riding her greatest danger. "The worst injury I've had on duty was when my mount threw his head back and charged straight up a cliff. His head crashed against my face and almost broke my nose. I saw stars and had to hang on for dear life. Behind me was nothing but a sheer drop with jagged rocks and scrub brush. After it was over, I had to have two stitches above my eye."

This explains two things. First, why a mounted officer must be highly skilled in horsemanship. Second, why the horse, despite its personality quirks, is chosen to patrol arduous terrain that automobiles or motorcycles could never execute.

The United States Park Police Mounted Unit was established in 1934 for one purpose—to patrol the streets and wooded areas of our nation's capital, Washington, D.C. The first unit could boast only one horse, rented from a local stable. Rock Creek Park, 1,900 acres of heavy woods in the heart of Washington, is crisscrossed with bridal paths that require special policing methods because the paths are narrow and unpaved. The horse seemed the answer. Not only could it travel winding trails with ease but a mounted officer could be spotted from a distance. This serves a double purpose—a help to those in trouble and a deterrant to the would-be criminal.

The Mounted Unit grew and increased its function. The uniformed officer and his handsome steed began to appear at national celebrations where there were masses of people, such as a presidential inauguration or the Cherry Blossom Festival. And what a visual asset they are! What American hasn't thrilled to the stately officer in dress uniform atop his shimmering horse?

During the demonstrations of the 1960's and 1970's, when large-scale violence erupted in Washington, officers and their horses were put to new tests—and passed. Weaving in and out of the angry throngs, the mounties were able to quell disturbances and reduce destruction. In fact, the mounted unit performed with such excellence that in 1973, the Washington operation was expanded to include two other immense urban parks, the Gateway National Recreation Area in New York City and the Golden Gate National Recreation Area in San Francisco.

When people ask Pepper how she got her job, she sums it up in one long, breathless sentence. "I applied, took the tests, waited eighteen months for an opening, was employed, went to Georgia for training, then worked rotating shifts in a patrol car for almost

Children throng to Pepper and her horse

Pepper (left) in dress parade

four years before I ever got a horse." This adds up to more than five years, but to Pepper, it didn't seem that long. She kept her eye on the goal, and the days marched by like soldiers in a dress parade. But to understand Pepper's attitude is to understand her parents.

Before he retired, Pepper's father was an anesthesiologist and an Army colonel who believed that you appreciate the good things of life more if you bring them about yourself. "We moved around a lot and always lived in big houses in nice neighborhoods," Pepper says. "But there were five children, and we were never showered with material things. My father always made us share, like the horse he gave us that Christmas. When we went to college, he made us work to help pay our way. And if we wanted a car, it was all right with him as long as we bought it ourselves."

Pepper's mother went along with the arrangements, although with considerably less enthusiasm than Mr. Karansky. He was affectionate and supportive but stern with his rules. Pepper found the sternness hard to deal with. Her friends down the street were allowed to date at 14, and when they turned 16 they were given automobiles of their own. Pepper was not allowed to date until she was 16, and she certainly was never given a car.

"You naturally compare yourself with your peers," Pepper says. "My peers had all sorts of things I never had, so I felt different from the crowd. I couldn't care less now. I finally got a VW, but it was because I bought it myself. It's old and beat-up now, but I still drive it and it's all I want. But when you're young and unsure of yourself, you see that you're different from your peers, and it shatters your self-image."

Pepper's worst years came during high school. "I went through a very trying period," she recalls. "I was too tall for my age. The boys in my class barely came to my chest. So when there was dancing, I never got danced with. That's pretty painful."

Pepper, who is now a trim 5'8" tall, says she "muddled" through those years somehow with the comfort of two or three other tall girl friends, and now she can laugh about her past. She's aware that everyone has painful experiences. She's also aware that such experiences can be turned into assets.

Such as her shyness. During her school years Pepper lived in seven different states—Georgia, Florida, Texas, California, Hawaii, Minnesota and Arizona. "Every two or three years, I was uprooted and had to start out on an entirely new set of circumstances and people," she says. "I had trouble making new friends. Mostly, I just stood back and was lonely."

But as a high school senior Pepper began examining herself and her shyness. If she stood back forever, she would not lead a very exciting life, she decided. She was letting the world dictate her experience rather than controlling it herself. "I wanted more than that," she says. "I wanted very much to live an interesting life, and I saw it all slipping by. I decided to do something about it."

After graduating from high school, Pepper left Phoenix to major in history at San Diego College, California. "I didn't know a soul there," she says, "but I made myself get out and meet people and join things. It wasn't easy. But I found that every time you make yourself do something like that, it gets easier the next time, and gradually your shyness just isn't a problem anymore."

Away from home, Pepper began to understand her parents and their restrictions, that they were preparing her and her siblings to live up to their potential, to meet challenges head-on.

"We became good friends then," she says. "I found I could tell them anything. They no longer made decisions for me, and they never judged. Even today they'll give advice if I ask for it, but they won't criticize if I don't take it."

As Pepper progressed deeper into her history studies, she discovered that she was not only interested in dates and events of the past but she was intrigued by the people who made them happen. She switched her major to social anthropology.

"I knew by then that I wanted a career that would involve working with people," she says. "That may sound strange from someone who had a terrific problem with shyness, but I had a big change in attitude during those years."

Pepper worked as a waitress during her college years, both in San Diego and in large resort hotels on Mackinack Island, Michigan, and was able to save some money. When she graduated, she immediately signed up for advance studies. Convinced that social anthropology was a crowded field and she'd need all the education she could manage just to land a job, she decided to get at least one graduate degree, maybe proceed to a doctorate. But her plans fell apart.

While in undergraduate school, Pepper had fallen in love with one of her professors. They went together for three years. But the professor married someone else.

"That was a real trauma," Pepper recalls. "I really felt torn apart. But, like all traumas, it made me grow. Looking back on it now I can honestly say I'm glad I didn't marry the professor and settle down in San Diego. I've had a much fuller life, but nobody could have told me that then."

Distraught, Pepper dropped out of graduate school to, as she calls it, "retrench" herself. She returned to Phoenix and for a few months worked in the fabric department of a large retail store. She lugged home yards of cloth and sewed till the wee hours of the morning. Under her mother's tutelage she learned intricate tailoring. "I'd spend a whole month tailoring just one jacket to perfection," she says.

Then she took a waitress job again. But nothing seemed to "feel right" for her. When her parents again moved to Hawaii, Pepper joined them. "I didn't do much of anything there," she says. "I can't explain what I was looking for. Perhaps it was just myself I hoped to find."

Still searching, Pepper moved to Washington, where she had friends, and took a job with the U.S. Department of the Interior, a secretarial job. She liked the work. It kept her mind off her problems, it satisfied her need to be around people, and it gave her an opportunity to learn how the government works. But the job failed to supply one criterion—a desire to work outdoors. "I felt all cooped up to the point of frustration," she says.

Her group at the time was working on a project to evaluate law-enforcement agencies within the department. This threw Pepper in touch with law-enforcement officers. She listened in fascination to what they said, asked questions and in the process found what she calls an important element in her life—a mentor.

"Everyone needs a mentor sometime in her life," Pepper says. "Someone who will help you, will take a personal interest without making demands. Sometimes it's a man, sometimes it's a woman. That doesn't really matter. What matters is that the mentor knows more than you and is willing to guide you."

Pepper's mentor was one of her bosses. He had previously served as a horse-mounted police officer with the New York City Police Department, had been a member of the U.S. Air Force and now held a responsible job with the Department of the Interior.

Because he felt Pepper was qualified for law enforcement, he shared with her the knowledge he brought from his experience. Pepper, already impressed with the law-enforcement officers she was working with, absorbed every morsel. When alone she digested what he said, weighed the information.

Would law enforcement supply all she wanted from a career? Certainly it would be a challenge, especially to a woman. Certainly she would be performing a useful service and dealing with a broad expanse of people. Certainly she'd be working outdoors. And, like a whipped cream topping, there was the possibility that she might be able to advance into the mounted unit, and she'd be back on a horse again!

Pepper applied.

Three departments within the U.S. government offer careers in law enforcement that interested Pepper because they deal with both people and nature—the Bureau of Land Management, the Wildlife Service and the U.S. Park Service. And each branch, now that new laws were in effect, would be hiring women. She sent applications to each, had interviews, took tests. And waited! There were 2,000 other applicants for the same jobs, many with a great deal of experience in related fields.

Sitting at her desk working on reports about law-enforcement officers, Pepper often visualized how different her life would be if she were an officer. But the months rolled by and still no word. She grew disappointed, dejected.

"If it weren't for my mentor, I guess I would have given up and looked for something else," she says. "He always knew the right thing to say to lift my morale. He just wouldn't let me quit hoping."

Finally, 18 months after she applied, Pepper got a call from the U.S. Park Service. She was hired! Not for the mounted unit, of course. That required at least three years of patrol duty first. But Pepper was on her way.

In January 1976, at the age of 28, Pepper entered the Federal Law Enforcement Training Center at Glynco, Georgia, for 18 weeks of fast-paced, hard-core training. There were 31 people in her class, three of them women.

The center was established in 1970 as a training facility for all federal police officers and criminal investigators with the exception of the Federal Bureau of Investigation (the FBI operates a separate facility at Quantico, Virginia). Located in the former Glynco Naval Air Station near Brunswick, the center functions from a flat, grassy campus and modern white buildings. Only a few miles away, the Atlantic Ocean laps at the shores of Georgia's scenic Sea Islands.

Pepper, now crisply dressed in her Class A uniform (black with blue stripe on the pants, blue shirt and tie, shiny black shoes), was captivated by the new world that lay before her. Suddenly she was learning subjects completely foreign to any she had studied in the past.

In law courses she learned general principles as they relate to investigation, detention, arrest, search and seizure. She learned what constitutes admissible evidence in court, the rights of individuals.

In communication she learned interviewing, presenting court testimony, how to write effective reports. In technique class she learned fingerprinting, photography, how to identify narcotics and how to collect and preserve criminal evidence.

In behavioral science she was taught social awareness, how to deal with people. She studied surveillance, handling informants, executing search warrants and working undercover operations.

Her classes were combined with "hands-on" practical exercises in which hired professionals played the roles of criminals and victims.

Pepper screeched a patrol car through a spin, made "arrests," handcuffed the offender, performed cardiopulmonary resuscitation and other exercises, all under the critical eyes of her instructors and classmates. She was graded on technique, criticized for her errors, then put through the paces again.

But the training that Pepper found most exacting was the instruction in firearms. "I'm just not into guns," she explains. "I never owned one, and the only time I ever shot in my whole life was with a .22 out on the desert once, shooting cans."

Pepper still doesn't like firearms. She prefers to rely on her skill in handling people rather than resorting to weapons. "People always think police officers are big on guns," she says. "Some of them are. But lots of them feel just as I do. The instructors on the range were excellent. They helped us deal with these feelings by teaching us to use the gun correctly and safely so that it becomes a tool rather than something to be afraid of."

Priscilla Pepper Karansky, Mounted Police 73

Three-dimensional targets designed for judgment shooting at the Federal Law Enforcement Training Center (photo courtesy FLETC)

For four weeks, Pepper averaged four hours every other day on the firing range. To learn stress methods she raced through an obstacle course—tunnel, ropes, hurdles and blocks—an unloaded shotgun in her outstretched arms. When she reached the firing point, she had to load and fire with split-second accuracy.

But learning *how* to shoot was not nearly enough. Pepper also had to learn how *not* to shoot. She worked with three-dimensional plastic people so real they could fool even the craftsmen who created them. These figures could be either friend or foe simply by substituting a camera or a flashlight for a knife or revolver. The action was lightning fast. Could Pepper the student determine in the wink of an eye whether the figure held a flashlight? Or was his finger pressing the trigger of a revolver?

As a further complication, the face could quickly be changed to that of an Oriental, a black, a Caucasian or a Latin with the use of double-stick tape. Again, would Pepper the student be influenced by race or ethnic origin?

Answers to these questions are all-important, for obviously law-enforcement officers in a free country must be devoid of prejudice, must exercise excellent and instant judgment.

"I know now that qualifying in firearms is one of my weaknesses in terms of technical skill," Pepper says. "I think it's important to try to be as good as you can, but it's more important to know that there are some things you are just not going to be good at. This was a hard lesson for me."

When her training at the center was completed, Pepper returned to Washington for her first assignment. She requested San Francisco and got it. For three years, she would serve in car patrol. If she proved good, she would then be eligible to apply for a transfer to the mounted unit.

"So I packed my little yellow VW and headed west," Pepper says. "To me it was like going home."

In New Mexico, her yellow bug broke down. The only mechanic in town was in charge of the bicentennial celebration in progress and wouldn't be available until it was over. Pepper rented a motel room and for five days watched the celebrants from the sidelines, wishing the merrymaking were over so she could be on her way. Almost three years had passed since she first applied for her new career, and she was anxious to begin. Before her stretched a challenge in a land of enchantment.

Golden Gate National Recreation Area is one of the most beautiful expanses of land in the United States and attracts more than 11 million visitors every year. Part of the area lies within San Francisco, part in the Marin County headlands across the bay. The two sections are stapled together by the famous Golden Gate Bridge. Golden Gate's collection of parks, its jungle of coastal redwood and oak trees, its cliffs and dunes and beaches and mountains and rivers spread themselves bountifully over 38,600 acres. Even Alcatraz, now empty but once the jail for some of the nation's most notorious criminals, is part of the park system.

Officers patrol the area in segments, 10 officers to the day shift, three to five at night. One week Pepper might be assigned the coastal area around Fisherman's Wharf. The next week she may comb the craggy cliffs where rock climbers and hang gliders gather. The prospects were intriguing, and Pepper was relieved when the celebration in New Mexico finally ended, the mechanic had repaired her auto and she could be on her way again.

Pepper's first few weeks in San Francisco were lonely ones. She knew no one and was reticent about making advances. Not because her shyness had returned, however. Quite the contrary.

Pepper was feeling good about herself and more self-confident than ever.

"I was just playing it cautious," she says. "I didn't want to make any big errors, to get started off on the wrong foot. I was the only woman there. They were sizing me up, and I guess I was sizing them up, too."

So she drove to work, put in the required hours, drove home. "I was changing shifts every two weeks," she says. "That plays havoc with your body. You have no social life at all. It's all work, work, work."

And there was another problem. For the first time in her career, Pepper was running headlong into discrimination. At school in Georgia she and the other two women had been all but ignored by their classmates. That wasn't too bad. The school would soon be over, and she and her classmates would be scattered across the country. But now she was on assignment and would face the prospect of discrimination almost every day. To make matters worse, Pepper was the first woman ever assigned to Golden Gate. Rumblings had begun even before she arrived.

Pepper on beach patrol

"I ain't riding with no woman," one officer declared in an off-the-record conversation.

This officer, as luck decreed, was the one Pepper was assigned to ride patrol with on her very first day of duty. He dashed to the patrol car, opened the door, helped her in. He took her to breakfast when the night shift was finished and insisted on buying. When Pepper couldn't cash a check because she was new in San Francisco, he opened his wallet and offered her its entire contents.

"He was a nice guy and would give you the shirt off his back," she says. "But even then he was treating me like a lady rather than a police officer. I didn't know till much later about the remark he had made earlier."

Pepper sensed that the other officers doubted her ability, and this bothered her. "I passed the same tests and took the same training," she says. "I wanted so much for them to like me, so I didn't say anything. I just kept plugging away, working hard and hoping that someday they'd accept me for what I was—a police officer."

When Pepper got into tight situations, the men would rush to "rescue" her, sometimes to her detriment.

"One time I stopped a car that was reported stolen," Pepper says. "I was positioned behind the vehicle door with my gun drawn, waiting for my backup, when an off-duty officer drove up in his personal car, leaped out in civilian clothes and yanked the driver out of the car. He had no gun and no handcuffs for the guy he yanked out, and he was in direct line of fire from the other passenger, who had his hand inside his coat and wouldn't move. He made it necessary for me to endanger my life and his in taking those two men into custody."

Despite the many times Pepper has proven herself, she feels she's still being put to task. "It's interesting that after five years they continue to check on me," she says. "When I go on a special case with a guy, the other officers will go to him later and ask how I did, how I fought, how I handled myself. I've never once heard them check on a man that way. They may in the locker room, but they haven't in my presence."

This does not bother Pepper the way it once did. She finds she no longer cares whether her coworkers like her. "It isn't my job to be liked," she says. "My job is to perform professionally and efficiently. That's what I try to do."

Although there is crime within the park—rape, armed assaults, homicide, drugs, thefts—Pepper's job is 85 percent public service, helping visitors in need.

"All sorts of things happen while they're in the park," Pepper explains. "They get lost, their cars may break down or be broken into, they may lose a child or get stranded on a cliff. Some of them even get marooned on a rock when the tide changes suddenly. And sometimes we're just asked where they can find a good restaurant. We try to prevent crime by being visible and within reach."

The three years of car-patrol duty sped by, and Pepper was finally eligible to apply for the mounted unit. She took the tests, scored well and was recommended by her superiors. For training she returned to Rock Creek Park in Washington, where she received 480 hours of intensive classroom instruction and riding experience.

For a starter she took horse psychology, first aid for horses, care of tack and the horse, parts of the horse and gaits. By the end of the third week, she was riding long trails in subfreezing temperatures. Then she advanced to crowd control and dressage (participating in parades). There were 15 students in Pepper's class. Only one other, Valerie Fernandez, was a woman. At graduation ceremonies, both women walked away with the only two class honors. Pepper topped all of her classmates in riding expertise; Valerie, now stationed at the park in New York City, won the academic award.

While Pepper was spending 480 hours in study, so were the horses. They were exposed to the usual distractions they are likely to encounter on the beat—flashing badges, exploding firecrackers, gunshots, sirens. They practiced walking across narrow bridges and through dark tunnels. Every year the horses must take a 40-hour refresher course at Fort Miley, California. Pepper returns to Glynco for her refresher course.

Unlike the original park police horse rented from a Washington stable, the horses now used are thoroughbreds who, for some reason, can no longer race or show. Their owners donate them to the U.S. Government as a tax writeoff. The upkeep per year is approximately $2,000 per horse, considerably less than the fee for operating a patrol car. Horses can serve about 15 years before they're retired. Patrol cars, on the other hand, are traded every year or two.

Although Golden Gate employs part-time grooms, Pepper

78 BREAKTHROUGH: *Women in Law Enforcement*

Pepper before a patrol

and the other mounted officers must assist in the care of the horses. Every day Pepper provides fresh water, hay, grain and salt. When it's her turn she mucks out the stalls, sweeps the aisles and blankets the horses. She helps keep the office and tack room orderly and free of fire hazards. And she grooms her mount every day. These duties, plus her written reports and her hours on patrol, round out a full 40- to 48-hour week.

Pepper's unit also participates in a community outreach program by appearing at schools and in parades on national holidays. "Public relations is one of our most important functions," Pepper says. "When you're on a horse, people just naturally gravitate to you. Sometimes I've had fifty school kids come running up. They'd probably go the other way if it weren't for the horse. They don't like the police, but after a while they're asking you questions, and pretty soon they begin to realize that police officers aren't such bad guys after all. Who knows, this may even keep some of them from embarking on a life of crime someday."

Physical stamina is important to Pepper's job, for often she's dealing with people much larger than she. Although she's taller than average, she weighs only 125 pounds. But she's been able to handle all of the physical aspects of her job.

"Oh, there are times when I wish I were six feet two inches tall and weighed one hundred seventy-five pounds," she says wistfully. "Like when we have a feed delivery at the barn and I'm unloading bales of hay that weigh eighty-five pounds each. But never when I'm dealing with people."

Keeping in shape makes Pepper feel good about herself. "That's very important," she says. "People react to you in a different way when you feel self-confident." To achieve this feeling, she lifts weights three times a week, runs 25 miles a week and has participated in two marathons.

Pepper shares with a girl friend a second-floor flat furnished in functional 18th-century oak antiques. In a sunny kitchen with a view of the Golden Gate Bridge, she blends a knowledge of Italian and French ("no heavy sauces") cooking to create gourmet dishes. Her favorite company dinner is a leg of lamb grilled in her own special way and served with polenta, herbed fresh vegetables and a dessert tart with Amaretto-flavored custard. One of her best friends is a caterer, and Pepper often elects to spend her spare time helping prepare festive food for weddings, parties and conventions.

Pepper running in Golden Gate Park

In other leisure hours, Pepper reads novels and how-to books on personal enhancement. She makes hand-sewn quilts, some of which she designs herself, and plays chess with her boyfriend. She dances, goes to bars where western and country music is featured, and pokes through second-hand stores for vintage clothes "with lots of beads."

Pepper feels women bring a special set of skills to a law-enforcement career. "Take paperwork, for instance," she explains. "We have mounds and mounds of it. Some men are excellent report writers, but most of them aren't accustomed to it, and they grumble constantly. Women seem to take it in stride."

And because women have been conditioned to different sensitivities, they can handle certain aspects of the job with more finesse than men do. "When I have to arrest a drunk, I don't just handcuff him and force him into a patrol car," she says. "I put my arm around him and explain exactly what is going to happen. I think he deserves to know. I've never yet had anyone I couldn't subdue without using macho tactics."

Pepper (left) and a friend cooking at home

Pepper offers five suggestions for women considering a career in law enforcement: learn self-defense and first aid, stay physically fit, become a good driver, read up on law and psychology and develop a sense of humor. "And I'd add one more," she says. "Find a mentor. It isn't always possible, but a mentor can help immensely."

Pepper, who would like to marry someday but does not intend to have children, feels a woman should examine very carefully the delicate balance between marriage and career. In order to advance, she will have to move often. Would her mate follow her? Would she refuse a promotion? Or give up the job?

And Pepper feels it's naive not to expect discrimination. "You just can't undo centuries of preconditioned prejudice in a few years," she explains. "Take it for what it is and rise above it. A woman will even face verbal abuse from other women. One refused to cash my check at a supermarket because she said I was depriving a man of a job."

Unlike the horse, Pepper is bent on improving the world around her, far beyond the reaches of park boundaries. Sometimes, when she's alone and working a design on a quilt, she goes over the pattern of her life and her career, her plans for the future.

Pepper is pleased that she's been able to use her persuasive verbal powers to get herself out of some tough situations. She feels it's her greatest asset. Only twice has she had to fire a gun in the line of duty, and both times it was to kill a wounded deer.

At Glynco last year, Pepper took a new course in hostage training. She was intrigued.

"The course wasn't designed for Strategic Weapons and Tactics (SWAT), the detail that goes in and physically rescues hostages," she explains. "This was a course in negotiating verbally with the hostage taker, so that we can avoid the sort of thing we had in Iran. Negotiating is a very important facet of international relations, and it's growing more important every year. That's what I have my eye on for the future."

"I have an overwhelming need to be needed. That's one good thing about this job. I know I'm needed here."

Elizabeth Aytes (Cookie) Kandler, Correctional Superintendent

COOKIE KANDLER SWITCHED ON THE LAMP AND LOOKED at the alarm clock. Ten minutes past 2:00, and she'd hardly slept a wink.

From down the hall drifted night sounds, soft as the tread of a kitten, of the other eight women who shared the house—a sigh, a cough, a turning. Cookie thought of them one by one. Karen, an arsonist. Bonnie, a larcenist. Noreen, an embezzler. Alice, check forger. Elaine and Mary Nell, both drug felons.

And Myra and Dana in the room next to Cookie's were murderers.

None of them wore handcuffs or any other physical restraint. There were no bars at the windows, the doors to their rooms were open, and the women were free to rise and roam at will. Collectively, they could ambush Cookie. For she was their one barrier to freedom, their prison warden.

Strangely, this knowledge, or the fear it could have triggered, was not what kept Cookie from sleep.

"I'm not the least bit afraid of these women," Cookie says later, squinting through a rising curl of smoke from her cigarette. "I know them. I know what I've got here. Out there on the street, I'd be frightened. But not here. Tomorrow night I'll sleep soundly."

Cookie never rests well on her first night away from home. Even on a pleasure trip, it takes a night or two to adjust to a dif-

The halfway house (photo by Elizabeth S. Smith)

ferent room, a bed other than her own. And this was a first night of sorts. Once every two months, although it is not required of her, Cookie signs up for a 48-hour shift, which means two days and two nights of constant duty without leaving the premises.

To Cookie, the women in the house constituted an assortment you could find in lots of places—a rooming house, a motel, a class at a community college. Karen was 19, the youngest. Myra was 63, the oldest. Some were white, some black—short, tall, fat, slender. They slept two or three to a room, their tabletops cluttered with family photos, nail polish and bottles of perfume. Elaine and Mary Nell lay curled like small children, sharing their pillows with a stuffed panda and a fluffy pink acrylic poodle.

The backgrounds of these women were varied and they had little in common. Yet there was one chain that linked them together like a strand of add-a-bead pearls. Each one had a memory she couldn't erase, a sound that hovered around the edges of her mind like the memory of a nightmare—the clang of a cell door that would separate her from the rest of the world. Each one knew the slow, tedious drag of days that eventually grew into years behind bars.

For all of them were convicted criminals, all had served time at women's prison in the state capital, and all were within six months of a parole hearing to determine if they could be set free. These last few months were being spent at a halfway house to prepare them for reentry into society.

How had these women arrived at this lovely two-story Tudor-style house on a tree-shaded boulevard in Charlotte, North Carolina, a church-going, bridge-playing town with a population of 400,000? How did Cookie, former beauty queen and debutante, now a 53-year-old grandmother, become a modern-day prison warden? And what exactly is a halfway house?

The answer to these questions involve three things—street crime, a cherished letter from a deceased grandmother and a change in the penal system.

"A halfway house is actually a Treatment Facility for Women," Cookie explains. "It's a deinstitutionalizing process, an opportunity for these women to learn skills, to live in a home atmosphere rather than getting out of prison one day and wham! Back on the streets the next. This is a critical period in their lives. The adjustment is hard. Some of them can't take it—they just go back to their old habits and land in jail again. Here we give them an opportunity to adjust in a caring atmosphere."

While these women were in prison, many changes have taken place in the outside world. Prices have skyrocketed, giant shopping centers have sprung up, drive-in banks have replaced downtown financial institutions. Microwave ovens and crock pots have invaded kitchens. And now they can make long-distance telephone calls without once talking with an operator.

"Many of them have never had a checking account," Cookie says. "They still carry their money around in their bras. Supermarkets confuse them, and they're astounded at today's prices."

So the halfway house was designed as an experiment. It's part of a softening in the penal system, a process that began a decade or so ago as an attempt to rehabilitate rather than punish. Even the vernacular has changed. A former prison warden is now, like Cookie, a superintendent of corrections. Guards have become correctional officers. While a prison unit such as this is called a halfway house, its inmates are known as residents.

"We're trying to get rid of old-fashioned terms," Cookie says. "Words like *warden* and *guards* and *inmates* always conjure up pictures of road gangs and striped uniforms, like the old Burt Reynolds movies."

Cookie is in favor of rehabilitation. It's not only more humane but it's also more practical. For one thing, rehabilitation saves tax money by reducing the number of repeaters. Jails are expensive.

But Cookie is ambivalent in her attitude. "I abhor the feeling I get every morning when I leave home and don't know if my silverware will be there when I get back," she says. "It infuriates me. Yet I have utmost sympathy for the women I work with here. I always think, There but for the grace of God go I. What would I have done in their shoes? If my children were starving, would I steal?" She pauses, crushes her cigarette in an amber-colored ashtray. "I think I would."

The halfway house in Charlotte was founded with federal funds in 1970. In 1978, the federal funds were withdrawn, but the house had been so successful that the state of North Carolina assumed its support. Cookie became superintendent in 1976.

Although the house is officially Prison Unit 4503, there is no sign on the well-tended lawn or on the house itself to indicate its purpose. Flanked on both sides by spacious homes, Prison Unit 4503 appears to passersby like the dwelling of a prosperous family.

And if it weren't for an occasional article in the local newspaper, even the next-door neighbors wouldn't know of its existence.

Inside on the lower floor there's a large parlor, a dining room with wide windows, a bright kitchen, an informal room equipped with stereo, color television, game tables and books. One room downstairs has been converted into offices for Cookie and her staff of three. Bedrooms and baths occupy the second story.

The house comfortably accommodates eight residents at a time. Each time a resident is awarded parole and moves out, Cookie becomes a "committee of one" to select a replacement. She drives 160 miles to Raleigh, the state capital, and there at the women's prison she carefully combs the records of every woman whose parole hearing is approaching. Records are kept in a large folder Cookie refers to as a jacket. Inside the jacket is a complete profile of the prisoner—case history, test results, arrest sheets, confinement papers, progress reports, work record. Cookie looks for clues as to how this woman will react and interact in a halfway house. Did she participate in any of the programs at prison or did she just sit there? Did she take advantage of work release? Sign up for secretarial courses? Readiness programs? Drug workshops? If she was not a high-school graduate, did she work on her general equivalency diploma, a study system for gaining a diploma without returning to school?

"All of these benefits were offered," Cookie explains. "If they didn't take advantage of them, then they wouldn't fit into a halfway house."

After her selection is made, Cookie rarely looks at the jacket again unless a special problem arises.

"I really push all that information way back in my mind and never think of the crime again," Cookie says. "I want to know each person as the individual she is today. I don't want any preconceived opinions. Sometimes after someone leaves and I'm closing out the files, I look back over the record and I'm flabbergasted. I can't believe that person did all those things."

Although in her own mind Cookie separates the individual from her crime, she handles it quite differently when she interviews the prospective resident. She asks each woman to tell in her own words what her crime was. Almost without fail the response is, "They *said* I did . . ."

"I stop her right on the spot," Cookie says. "Her first grip on reality is assuming responsibility for her crime. She must say, 'I robbed a Handy Pantry' or 'I killed a man.' She must *admit* doing wrong. Then her rehabilitation can begin."

Cookie explains to the prospect what life at the halfway house is like. As in all prisons, the restrictions outweigh the privileges. But in a halfway house, another dimension is added. Once the new resident enters the door she begins assuming responsibility for her own life, a responsibility that, until that minute, was in the hands of uniformed officials.

First of all, she must work. Cookie allows the new resident 30 days in which to find a job, but she's left to her own devices as to how she goes about this.

"We'll assist her, of course," Cookie explains. "We'll make suggestions, and we'll steer her clear of any employers who won't hire prisoners on work release. But these women must make their own job plans."

The residents read want ads, fill in applications, telephone for an interview and are required to tell the prospective employer of their prison record. On the job they cannot leave their place of employment during working hours, cannot receive visitors or telephone calls. They must ride the city bus, which passes the halfway house on regular schedules, and must go directly to and from work without deviating, not even to duck into a drugstore for a Coke or candy bar.

"I tell them right off to get an alarm clock," Cookie says. "In prison they were told when to get up, when to eat breakfast, when to go to bed. Here they're on their own. If they oversleep, that's their problem. I won't call in and make excuses for them, and I won't drive them to work to get them there on time."

Other than routine inquiries, Cookie never checks on the resident at work. She wants her to know she trusts her. There's one exception, however. If the resident reports she is being harassed, Cookie shows up immediately.

"That's one thing I won't put up with," Cookie says. "Not from an employer or from other workers. These women are to be treated with respect and courtesy. If they don't get it, I tell them to resign and look for another job. Then I won't let another of our residents work at that place again."

The residents find jobs in offices, short-order food chains, restaurants and in construction. They ring up cash registers, handle money, have access to company records.

"Most of the employers are glad to get them," Cookie says.

"They're reliable. The employers know they'll arrive on the job, put in the hours and stay six months. For food franchises like Hardee's or McDonald's, that's great. Their turnover is so rapid, they're happy to get someone who'll stay that long."

Out of her earnings, each woman must pay $5 per day to the halfway house. If she has children she must send support money back home. She's allowed $5 per week for transportation and $20 per week spending money. The balance is placed in a fund, which draws interest like a savings account, and is returned to the worker when she is paroled.

"Some of them leave here with as much as $2,000 accumulated, enough to start a new life," Cookie explains. "And they're learning that they can't freeload, they're learning to assume responsibility for their own children, and they're learning the value of saving. It's a good program."

Housekeeping responsibilities are divided equally among the residents. Cleaning, cooking and shopping chores are rotated from week to week. Dana may scrub the bathrooms this week. Next week she may vacuum the parlor or cook supper.

The women prepare one hot meal a day and serve it early in the

Cooking chores are shared at the halfway house (photo by Elizabeth S. Smith)

evening on an oval table beneath an elegant, sparkling chandelier. Menus are planned a week in advance by the cooks for the week in order to give the shoppers a list of needs. They budget, just as a family would budget. But on Sunday, they'll splurge and have something special—a pot roast or strawberry shortcake.

"Sometimes they goof off," Cookie says. "If I come in and find dirty glasses in the sink, I give them warning. If I come in the next day and find it the same way, I suspend all passes and telephone privileges."

The residents grumble. "Gol-lay, Mrs. Kandler, that's not fair," they say. "We didn't *all* leave the sink dirty."

"I tell them to find out who's goofing off and to correct the situation themselves," Cookie says. "Until then, they all pay the price."

After one such session with a happy ending, one resident said to Cookie, "Oh, Mrs. Kandler, you're so sweet."

"*Sweet*, I'm not," Cookie responded. "*Fair*, I try to be."

Each resident is allowed limited passes to visit her family or to go to a movie, church or dinner with an approved community

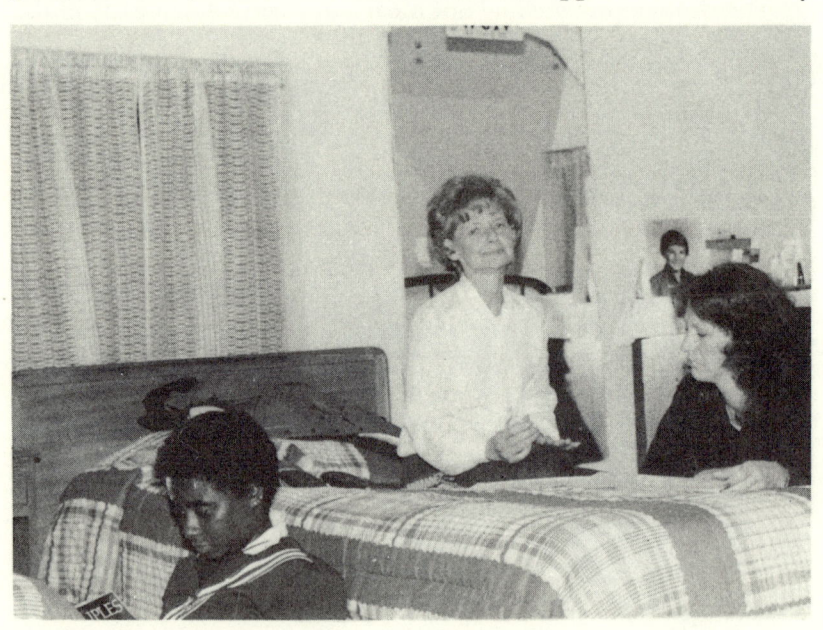

Residents relaxing in their room (photo by Robert H. Morrison)

volunteer. All other excursions, such as a trip to the grocery store or a shopping spree, must be in the company of Cookie or one of the staff counselors.

Long before Cookie finishes explaining the routine, the prospective resident is intrigued. How different it will be from cell life! The day she entered prison, all personal identification was removed—driver's license, credit cards, name tags, photos. She was whisked to the reception room, where she was stripped and sprayed with disinfectant. There were no doors on the bathrooms, no privacy curtains at the toilet or shower stalls.

"That's hard on a woman," Cookie says. "Right off, she begins to lose self-respect and any sense of personal identity. Soon she hides behind prison nicknames—Yo-Yo, Slick, Speed, names like that."

At the halfway house, Cookie insists that the women drop their prison nicknames. They can surround themselves with items that mark their own individuality—snapshots, makeup, small trinkets from home. There are closets for their clothes and doors at the bathrooms.

"One new girl was so enthralled she took three baths the first day," Cookie recalls. "Almost immediately, you can see a difference. They begin to respond to their own identity, to feel like a person again."

But regaining self-respect after a prison experience takes much longer, Cookie says. It's a slow process that develops one day at a time. Cookie or a staff member is available around the clock for consultation or just plain conversation. A special relationship develops. Most of the women accept this, but there are always a few who are reluctant.

"This doesn't mean anything," they scoff. "You're just paid to be nice to me."

But as the weeks roll by, these few doubters find that it's more than that.

Cookie maintains a fine line, as delicate as a spider web, between residents and herself. They must understand that she is boss and always has the final word. Behind her back they call her "Chief" or "Sergeant." Some like her, some don't. But Cookie isn't concerned with their affection. She just wants their respect.

"One came in the other day after getting her first job and hugged me," Cookie says. "That's enough for me."

* * *

Cookie, whose nickname makes her sound more like a television starlet than a correctional superintendent, arrived in her position via a spiraling path that began with a broken marriage. Along the way, she was inspired by the optimism and courage of her grandmother.

Gadsden, Alabama, was home for Cookie, but she spent summers and holidays with her grandparents in Tasso, Tennessee, a tiny town that most maps ignore.

"I admired Mam-maw tremendously," Cookie says. "She just about ran that little farm community. Everyone came to her with all their problems. She put on a Christmas pageant every year and filled a bag with fruit and nuts for every child there. Sometimes it was the only present they got."

Actually Mam-maw was postmistress. When the daily train chugged to a stop, Cookie rushed out to drag the mailbag into the one-room post office. It wasn't a heavy bag, of course—a few letters, mail-order catalogs and newspapers, and occasionally a small package rolling around the bottom. But it gave Cookie a sense of contributing—and an excellent excuse to be with Mam-maw. At other times, Cookie thumbed a ride on horse-drawn ice wagons, played in the creek, romped through woods, always storing up memories to take home to the polished apartment in Gadsden.

From Mam-maw, Cookie developed her "little-engine-who-could" philosophy. "You know that old story about the little engine chugging up a steep hill and finally making it because it changed its tune from 'I think I can' to 'I know I can'," Cookie says with a twinkle. "That's helped me through a lot of tough spots in my life."

The worst was when her marriage broke up. With two small daughters, Debby and Susan, to raise single-handedly and with only child-support checks for income, Cookie knew she'd have to go to work. But where? At the University of Tennessee she had majored in education, but she had married her college sweetheart the summer after graduation and never worked.

"We were the typical rah-rah kids," Cookie says. "Bob was fraternity president and popular on campus. I was the beauty queen. We started dating when we were freshmen, and we went together all through college. You'd think we'd make the perfect couple."

Elizabeth Aytes (Cookie) Kandler, Correctional Superintendent 93

Cookie as a college beauty queen

After their wedding Bob and Cookie zipped off to Chillicothe, Ohio, for Bob's first job. There the trouble began.

"It took me six months just to learn to spell Chillicothe." A smile creases Cookie's face, then disappears. "By then we found we just had nothing to talk about since we weren't flitting to sporting events or fraternity dances. But in six months, I was pregnant so I put my mind on having a baby."

Two years later, they moved to Charlotte and had a second daughter. Bob was a young executive on the rise. Socially, they were popular. They joined civic clubs and worked at community projects. Bob became vice-president of the Jaycees, Cookie was president of the Jaycettes. They became the youngest couple to be admitted to the country club of their choice.

"People who saw us on weekends thought we were the happiest couple in town," Cookie says. "But from Monday till Friday, we had nothing to talk about."

Caring for Debby and Susan consumed Cookie's time until the children entered kindergarten. Then Cookie confronted empty hours with no challenge. Bob had his business, the children had schools and Cookie had housework.

"I'd be scrubbing the kitchen floor and I'd say to myself, 'You mean you got a college education for this?'" Cookie says. "If I could have foreseen then what would happen to our marriage I could have made a career for myself then. But this was an era when you stayed home and raised your kids unless you absolutely had to work."

After the breakup Cookie began her career as a Welcome Wagon hostess. In this job she could schedule her hours so she'd be home after school. From this she progressed to receptionist at a doctor's office, an insurance claims processor, educational director for the Heart Association, a personnel agent, sales director for a hotel, and service coordinator for a motel chain.

In 1975, after Susan and Debby were grown, Cookie married another Bob. This time the wedding was quite different from the traditional formalities of her first marriage. They married in a small chapel and wrote their own vows: "You are my beloved and you are my friend and we shall live together as long as we both shall love."

When Cookie reentered the job market, she set her sites on a different type of employment. From her earlier jobs she had learned that she required two aspects from a career. First, she must deal with people rather than facts and figures and inanimate objects. Second, she must be needed and perform an important service.

The first job that satisfied both requirements was as public education field officer for the prison system.

"Actually it's a public relations job," Cookie explains. "I worked for all prison units within a 10-county area. I went to schools, civic clubs, radio and television stations telling the public what the Department of Corrections was doing."

She helped set up advisory boards, prepared brochures and press releases. And learned quickly that the public does not know what's happening in the penal system. When she spoke to junior-high students, all they wanted to know was "What are they in there for?" When she visited a woman's club they asked, "What about the children?" And when she addressed a men's club, they quizzed her about how much it was costing the taxpayer.

From this job Cookie moved upward to probation parole and became the first woman in North Carolina to take over an all-male case load.

"I had one hundred thirty-eight convicted criminals, all males, to supervise," Cookie says. "Some were parolees and some were on probation. I had to make sure they were living by the rules. And I had to be there when they needed help."

Her first daily chore was to read the police department's arrest sheet from the night before. If any of her parolees were listed, she visited them in jail, learned the details of their arrest, made sure they were fairly represented. She checked regularly on the others and kept an up-to-date file on each. "I'd make home visits to see if everything was going all right there," Cookie says. "I telephoned employers for a progress report. If they were missing, I'd have to go round them up. Sometimes, I'd have to go undercover to the gosh-awfulest places you can imagine. There were never enough hours in the day."

Parolees and probationers, according to Cookie, can be lumped into three divisions. At the top are the ones who'll go straight. They've learned their lessons, they've paid their price, and they'll never commit another crime. At the bottom are the incorrigibles, the repeaters to whom crime is a way of life.

"But in the middle are the ones who could go either way," Cookie says. "Those are the ones I worked with most."

When Cookie was offered her present job she was skeptical.

Birthday celebration at the halfway house (photo by Robert H. Morrison)

"I had served on the board here at the halfway house," she says. "I knew already this was a burn-out job. That's why the other woman was leaving. There's so much stress, and you're subject to call any hour of the day or night. And so much heartache. I wasn't sure I could take it."

But Mam-maw's "little engine who could" now had a caboose—a letter marked "to be opened after my death."

The letter was tucked in a stack of yellowed newspapers in a well house off the back porch of Mam-maw's old home. It was written on ruled tablet paper and addressed to Cookie, then age four. It spoke of Mam-maw's love for her granddaughter, of how she wanted Cookie to be always safe and secure even though "it's so easy for those little hands to reach for the wrong things, those little feet to go down the wrong path."

Cookie pulled out Mam-maw's letter and reread it. She thought of other grandmothers who wanted the same things for their granddaughters, of the pain they must feel when they learn that little hands had reached for the wrong thing or little feet had gone down the wrong path.

She took the job.

Now Cookie's outreach is much farther than the job demands. She's scheduled to work 40 daylight hours a week, with nights and weekends off, but she's often summoned to solve a dispute, and she chooses to spend one weekend on duty every other month.

Cookie plans programs for the residents in their off hours, invites bankers in to teach about checking accounts, sets up workshops in planned parenthood and drug problems, holds classes in crafts and needlework. "I just want them to know there are better things in life than hanging out at the local beer joint," she says.

Cookie plans birthday celebrations for all the residents and Mother's Day parties for those with children. "One year every resident was a mother," Cookie says. "We made corsages, got out linen tablecloths and silver candlesticks, invited their children, wore long dresses and served 30 Cornish hens. We wouldn't let the residents do one bit of work. The board members even washed dishes."

Another year Cookie fixed Caesar salad, and her husband prepared his specialty, beef strogonoff. "And you wouldn't believe Christmas," Cookie says. "We decorate two trees up to the ceiling, loaded with gifts. We invite their families. People in the community give me money to buy presents. Clubs and church groups bring stuffed stockings. It's great!"

Meanwhile, Cookie disciplines fairly but firmly. "Discipline is a form of love," she explains. "I disciplined my own daughters, and I discipline these women here."

There are failures at the halfway house—women who refuse to respond or those who have infractions and must be returned to prison. These failures weigh heavily on Cookie. Like Corinne, who "came in like a whipped dog—stringy blond hair, messy, stooped over." Corinne did well at the halfway house, won her parole and left to begin a new life in Charlotte. "Corinne came from a small town known to have one of the highest crime rates in the country," Cookie says. "Jail is a way of life to a whole segment of that community. They'd kill for a six-pack. So I asked that a condition of the parole state that she is not allowed to return to that town."

But it didn't work. Within 30 days Corinne was pecking meekly at the door of the halfway house. Her clothes were torn, her arms and legs bruised and her appearance worse than ever.

"I just couldn't give up on her," Cookie says. "I persuaded her parole officer to let me have one more chance. I got her room and her job reinstated, but in less than 30 days she was downhill again. Now she's back in prison. Some people are like that. They just need to be institutionalized. I feel I gave her the best opportunity she'll ever have, but I'd never under any circumstances let her come back here again. There are too many others in prison just waiting for a chance like this. It's their turn."

Cookie feels a great sense of failure in Corinne's case—another burn-out reaction. She tries to dwell on the success stories. Like Lauri, a drug offender, who now holds a responsible position with a loan company in Atlanta, Georgia. And Donna, who met a man while on work release, married him after she was paroled and now has a home and a good life.

One of Cookie's greatest frustrations springs from the fact that the policies and procedures for prison (they're bound in what she calls the "big red book") were written for men in a 160-man prison unit.

"They laugh at us at state headquarters and call us the Holiday Inn or the country club," Cookie says. "The policy makers just don't know what to do with us as far as regulations are concerned. We don't fit the pattern, but they're unwilling to change any of the rules."

Cookie with daughters Debby (left) and Susan (right) at Christmas (photo by Phil Flanary)

The red book stipulates, for instance, that there must be one staff member for every five inmates when prisoners are taken away on some mission. All cleaning equipment must be locked up when not in use. There must be no glass containers on the premises.

"Those rules won't work here," Cookie explains. "Our women ride the bus on their own. We can't lock up cleaning equipment because this is a home. We need the oven cleaner and the ammonia right here on the pantry shelf. And we let our women have perfume in bottles. We constantly have to account to the state for these infractions."

Cookie, fun-loving and gregarious, deals with stress by engaging in an active social life. She and Bob have a swimming pool at their home and a condominium at a South Carolina beach. Bob is president of a social club called Advocates of Good Times, and Cookie serves on the board. With the club they dash off to ski on weekends, to attend steeplechases or go to the shore. Cookie and

Cookie packing after a night at the halfway house (photo by Elizabeth S. Smith)

Bob also belong to an overseas travel club, which takes them to exotic places such as Martinique, Mexico, the Bahamas and Haiti.

But Cookie's greatest joy is close to home—her granddaughter, Britt. Both Debby and Susan are married and live nearby. Family gatherings are frequent and joyful. And every week Cookie sets aside an hour or two to spend alone with Debby's daughter, her only grandchild.

A prime requirement for a job such as Cookie's is maturity, which Cookie defines as "the ability to make judgments and decisions without emotion."

"And she's got to know what street crime is like," Cookie says. "A degree in criminal justice or psychology or sociology just won't do it, although they're good subjects to take, and she'll need a degree just to keep the agency from deciding in favor of a man. But she needs to take an entry-level position in probation and parole or as a case analyst in a diagnostic center. If she learns all she can and assumes responsibility, then her superiors will begin to notice her. Promotions in law enforcement come mainly through merit anyway."

When Cookie reports to her job, she's neither armed nor frightened. There are handcuffs in a desk drawer, but she has never even removed them from their box. On the nights she spends at Prison Unit 4503, Cookie removes her rings and watch and leaves them on her bedside table in plain view. Her purse, with cash and credit cards and sometimes a piece of jewelry, is dropped "anyplace." And she's never missed a thing.

"That tells me something," she says with conviction. "The concept is working."

and others who excel

Geraldine Anderson Lawrence, Border Patrol Agent

WHEN GERRI LAWRENCE REPORTED TO DUTY AS A Border Patrol agent in McAllen, Texas, in 1976 she was referred to as "the nigger lady." When she left two years later, she was respectfully known as "Miss Lawrence."

McAllen is one of a number of rural farm communities scattered along the Rio Grande, the historical river that separates the United States from Mexico. The area is infested with illegal aliens who swarm in over the water in any manner they can—dog paddling, swinging from huge tractor inner tubes, rowing in handmade boats. The Mexican aliens arm themselves with rocks, ice picks, brass knuckles and farm tools. They forge illegal papers, then sign up to work for a pittance at farms and ranches —anything to stay on the American side of the river. But they're in the country illegally, and they know it. And it's up to the Border Patrol to deal with them.

The Border Patrol operates under the U.S. Immigration and Naturalization Service of the Department of Justice and is charged with the task of keeping the borders of our country secure. About 4,000 miles of borderland stretch along the Canadian boundary, about 2,000 miles along Mexico and another 2,000 miles along the Gulf of Mexico. Because the territories are so different, so are the methods of operation. The specific duties of the agents involve preventing smuggling and illegal entry. And they must detect and apprehend illegal aliens already inside the country.

To accomplish this, agents set up checkpoints for vehicles, they search trains, planes, buses and ships. They operate electronic sensors so sensitive that even the movement of underground roots in high wind will trigger a signal. Extremely mobile, the agents use motorcycles for sandy areas, horses for mountain terrain, jeeps in canyons and gorges, boats in lake regions and large vans when they need to transport a group of aliens to headquarters. Backup agents often use helicopters and single-engine airplanes.

Gerri was working as a travel agent in New York City when she first applied for a job with the Border Patrol and took the required tests. About a year later, while conducting a tour in the Caribbean, she received word that she was to report to duty in three weeks. As a divorced mother of two young sons, Gerri had to make some quick arrangements before rushing off for 16 weeks of intense physical and academic training at the Border Patrol Academy in Los Fresnos, Texas (the course is now conducted at the Federal Law Enforcement Training Center, Glynco, Georgia).

At Los Fresnos, she took courses that stretched both her mind and her body. She studied Spanish, criminal law, laws that relate to immigration and nationality, evidence and court procedures, firearms, fingerprinting, report making and the methods of operation within the Border Patrol. Soon she was running one mile in eight minutes, scaling seven-foot walls, doing 20 push-ups and executing a strenuous obstacle course.

The first assignment for all Border Patrol agents is the Mexican border. When Gerri arrived at McAllen, she was exuberant about her career. But McAllen boasted a population of 70,000, only 20 of which were black. She was not only the first black agent to serve the area but she was also the first woman.

"Sometimes I'd walk into a field of workers to check their papers and the whole field would light up with the word 'nigger.' Not to my face, of course," she says. "Always to my back."

And she even suffered the abuse of other agents who felt that the Border Patrol wasn't the place for a woman. But with guts and determination, she showed them. She splashed into the murky waters of the Rio Grande in hot pursuit of fleeing aliens, engaged in some rapid foot chases through brambles and barbed wire and endured lots of scratches and scars and torn clothes.

Once while patrolling the port of entry near Hidalgo, Texas, Gerri radioed headquarters that she had sighted a group of aliens. "Sending backup," headquarters replied. "Don't bother," Gerri radioed. "There are *only* six, and I have them in custody." *Only* six, indeed!

Gerri Lawrence in uniform

"I heard lots of comments about that later," Gerri says. "But I don't think they ever doubted my ability again."

Gerri now is stationed near San Diego, California, in the most heavily violated area on the entire border. There the aliens cross the border through mountains and canyons. And again they work mostly on farms and ranches.

When Gerri was being shown her new assignment, the Chula Vista Sector, by her partner, they received a radio message that a group of 60 aliens had just "busted" (scattered) through the mountains. Gerri and her partner jumped from their bus and scurried up the slopes.

"I didn't know a thing about the terrain," she recalls. "But I used my expertise in circumvention, and the two of us chased that group up one side of the mountain and down the other right into the waiting hands of the El Cajon Station Unit. When I came out of the mountain, you should have seen the looks on the faces of the men who manned the station. I was the first female agent they had ever encountered in this manner."

Many aliens in the California area live in the canyons. They build makeshift houses (called *hootches*) of plywood, cardboard or plastic. Sometimes they just dig holes in the side of mountains to protect themselves from the elements. They live with no running water, no garbage disposal, no toilets.

"You can imagine what the mess is like when we're working at night and walk into a hootch," Gerri says. She has at times, by combing every mountain cavity, routed out as many as 80 aliens in one night.

"They'll hide anywhere," she explains. "Once I was checking a chicken ranch and found a foot sticking out from under a pile of fecal matter. An alien had dived under that pile but couldn't get his foot hidden fast enough. He smelled so bad even the other aliens wouldn't get close to him."

Gerri carries a .357 Magnum pistol and wears two types of uniforms—a "rough duty" outfit for the hard jobs, a dress uniform for meeting the public. She's also worked undercover with city patrol, dressing in plain clothes and posing as a salesperson. "I was able to pick up information leading to the prosecution of a number of frauds and smugglers," she says.

And she's learned to spot a car or truck with illegal aliens aboard. "You get so you can tell how a car looks with a load, how

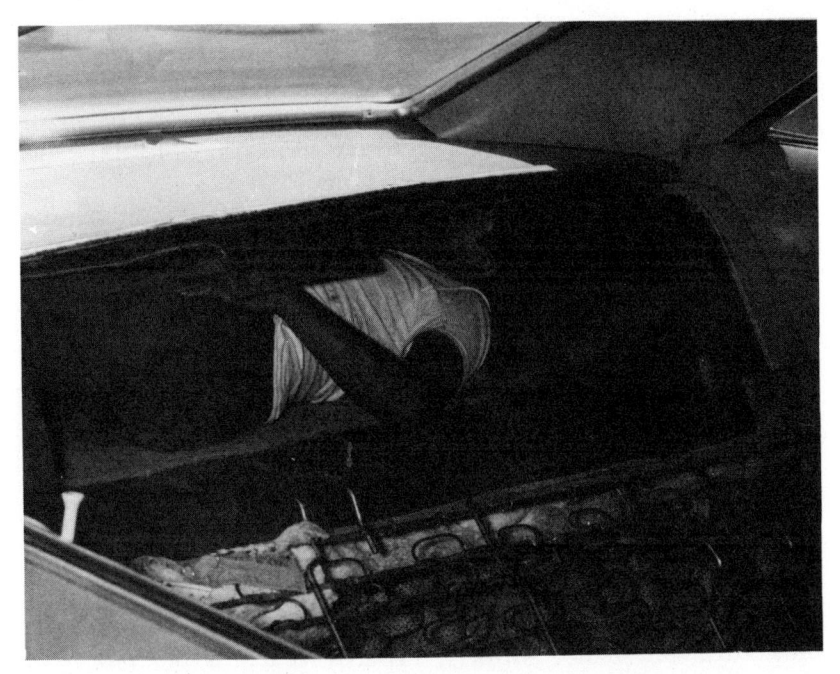

An alien hiding in a compartment of a 1966 Chevrolet

the driver reacts," she says. "We find aliens stowed away under car seats, in the trunk, on racks underneath the car, even up under the hood."

Gerri grew up in Jersey City, New Jersey, and worked in New York City before joining the Border Patrol. Although a college degree is not necessary for her job, Gerri has studied at the American Institute of Banking, Chase Secretarial School, Meridian Business School and the Ophelia De Vore Charm School, all in New York City. She has begun college courses at Miramar College in San Diego and plans to get a degree in criminal justice when her sons are older.

Gerri and her sons share a four-bedroom condominium in Santee, California. Although she averages 50 working hours a week on rotating shifts, she manages to find time to read, refinish antiques and cook. But most of her off-duty hours are spent in mothering. With her sons she fishes, plays ball, chess, checkers, backgammon and electronic games. For two years, she coached her sons' basketball teams, and she's regularly in the stands rooting for them when they're on the baseball diamond.

In February 1982, Gerri chalked up another credit when she was assigned the position of temporary supervisor. She's the first black to hold the position, the third female.

In the Border Patrol Gerri, now in her thirties, can advance to the position of criminal investigator or as deportation officer. She has her eye on the former.

Susan Marie Stanton, Jailer

BY NIGHT SUSAN STANTON, TRIM AND RADIANT IN BRIGHT pink tutu and ballet slippers, expertly practices her *temps de flèche*.

By day, in heels and street clothes, she walks unarmed and unafraid among rapists, thieves and murderers. Susan is a jailer. In more euphemistic terms, her title is Director of Corrections for the Jackson County, Missouri, Prison. She's the first woman to hold the job and probably the only ballerina who ever will.

The jail, located in Kansas City, holds 500 inmates, all male. Like most prisons, the Jackson County unit is drab, overcrowded and uncomfortable. In summer, the inside temperature soars above 100 degrees Fahrenheit; in winter the cells are dank and chilly. Naturally, the prisoners grumble and complain, hurling obscenities at one another and at the guards.

But when Susan walks along the rails, the inmates assume a different attitude. They may not all like her, for she's their barrier to freedom. But it's obvious they respect her. The respect, however, was not a gift. They made Susan earn it.

The first test came on a bleak day in October 1977. Susan was 27 and new at the job when she received word that one housing tank was in an uproar. "It was one of our most aggressive tanks

Left: Susan at a jail cell *Right: Susan at ballet practice*

and the one that caused the most problems," Susan says. "There were thirty-two men in the unit, so we decided to split them up and move them out of the area."

But the prisoners would have none of it. They armed themselves with mop wringers and TV antennae, turned on water spigots and flooded the cells. Then they ran electrical wires to the metal bars so that anyone touching the metal would get a jolt of electricity. "Those hot bars had quite a punch," Susan recalls. "And standing in three feet of water made it dangerous."

Susan summoned the tactical squad, 35 men highly trained to quell prison disturbances. In helmets and armored vests, the men tried their persuasive powers and failed. Then they threw tear gas, but the prisoners used wet towels to protect their faces. Two hours later, the situation remained the same. The rioters refused to budge.

Then Susan, in dress and heels and armed only with a gas mask, walked to the area and put an end to the crisis.

"I didn't say anything the tactical force hadn't already said," she recalls. "I simply asked them very quietly to please come out and lay down their arms."

They did.

Whether it was Susan's charm or her lack of force, the prisoners decided Susan's compassion was something to respond to. It still works. When there are grievances, Susan is at the rails, taking notes, asking questions—and getting results. The prisoners know they're being listened to. To most of them, that's more important than a new cell or a TV set.

"But they know I'm no patsy," Susan says. "If push comes to shove, I have no qualms about throwing gas into the cells or having someone physically removed from the tank. I won't stand at the rail and beg."

Susan grew up in what she calls an "upper-middle-class" family in Kansas City, led a sheltered life and certainly had no knowledge of street crime. She rose to her position through the ranks. In 1972, she began work as a clerical employee in the same jail. But she felt unchallenged. With a B.A. degree in political science from the University of Santa Clara, California (she graduated cum laude), an M.A. in the same subject from the University of Houston, Texas, and as a recipient of a National Science Foundation Fellowship, Susan looked for ways to step up the ladder.

When a new Department of Corrections was established, she talked herself into a job in jail management. "I just had the guts to speak up and ask for it, and nobody said no," she says. As head of the Division of Management Services, she worked with both inmates and staff members, learning the intricacies of prison management. In 1977, when the top job became available, Susan got the appointment.

"I'm not a cold person," Susan explains. "I can't live around these people and know about things like rape and sodomy and murder without hurting inside. But I believe in punishment. These prisoners are in jail because that's where they belong, but I can still find something good in every one of them."

Susan's compassion shines in what she terms "small" ways. She has no intention of making prison life pleasant, but she tries to make it as "normal" as possible. She arranged to have wall clocks installed. She schedules an occasional concert. She's seen that meals were improved, and even added special fare for the holidays. And she has expanded visiting privileges to include children.

But the greatest improvement is less tangible. Susan has made certain that her staff of 200, which she supervises, is a caring staff that will listen to prisoners' complaints. Morale has improved, tension has lessened.

Susan is single and lives alone in her own home. With staff and committee meetings, interviewing prospective employees, making speeches to civic clubs and organizations, she has precious little time to devote to friends and family. But she feels the need to unwind, so five nights a week she dances with a semiprofessional ballet company in Kansas City.

There, to the soothing strains of Tchaikovsky or Mendelssohn, Susan can wipe out for a few hours her daily exposure to what is often called a living hell.

Kathryn Harper Morris, Airport Security Agent

FOR MOST PEOPLE, AVIATION SECURITY BEGINS AND ENDS at the X-ray checkpoints within the airport terminal. For Kathryn (Kathy) Morris, it's quite another story.

As Special Agent in the Air Transportation Security Division of the Federal Aviation Administration (FAA), Kathy daily assumes responsibility for enforcing federal security regulations at the largest (in area) airport in the entire world—Hartsfield Atlanta International Airport in Georgia. On its busiest days, more than 100,000 people pass through the terminal.

Although the familiar checkpoints are only a fraction of Kathy's duties, they alone could keep her hopping. "Last year, more than one hundred people attempted to pass through the passenger-screening checkpoints with concealed weapons," she says. That means over one hundred cases she must investigate, interrogate and decide whether to prosecute through the FAA's legal department or merely reprimand.

Kathy is the first woman to hold this position in Atlanta.

114   BREAKTHROUGH: *Women in Law Enforcement*

Although she wears no uniform and carries no gun, it's her job to see that all federal regulations regarding airport security and safety are carefully enforced. Security measures are stringent now because of the rash of airplane hijackings in 1970-71. At first, the Department of Transportation tried to deal with the menace by assigning deputized sky marshals to fly on high risk flights.

Kathy was a secretary with the FAA when the sky marshal program was announced. Although she was a petite 5'4'' tall and only 25 years old, she was convinced she could serve as expertly as a man. And the exhilaration of performing a great service far outweighed the obvious dangers involved.

As part of the required sky-marshal training, Kathy was sent to the Federal Bureau of Investigation (FBI) Academy in Quantico, Virginia, where she learned self-defense and the use of firearms. She was the only woman in her class, the smallest member—and graduated with top honors.

Kathy was then assigned to the security staff in Atlanta and waited a call to the sky. But the call never came. Most of the sky-marshal program was dropped in 1974 when officials determined that the way to prevent hijackings is within the terminal rather than in the sky.

But Kathy's training at the FBI Academy paid off, and she began the climb to her present position. First she was appointed civil aviation security inspector for 13 airports in North and South

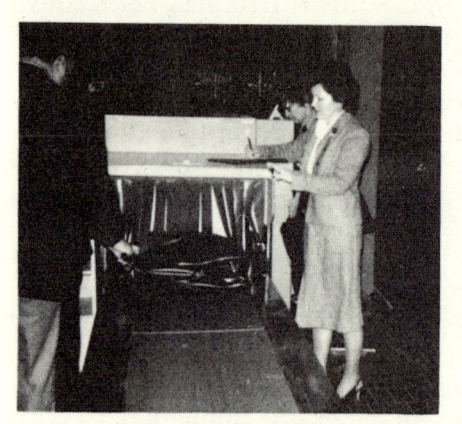

Left: Kathy checking an X-ray device
Right: Kathy consulting with a local police officer

Carolina, the first woman in the south to attain the job. Traveling out of Atlanta, Kathy covered up to five airports each week, carefully checking their security measures, then returned to Atlanta for weekends.

As a woman, Kathy felt "on display" every time she executed her job, but she was determined to succeed. She never asked for special favors or assistance. She continued to work when she felt ill or when there were pressures at home.

"All the airport managers were men," Kathy says. "At first they were put off when I came in to check their security." But Kathy gradually won their acceptance and approval. When the position in the mammoth new Atlanta terminal opened in 1980, Kathy won the appointment.

Her list of duties is awesome. She plans, develops and conducts a continuous safety program from her office within the terminal. She provides technical assistance to air carriers and airport management. She conducts inspections of hazardous materials being shipped by air. She runs tests on X-ray devices, checks to be sure the personnel is properly trained. No two days are alike. Even a tiny break in a fence or a loose hinge on a gate is her responsibility.

On a recent day, a baggage handler lifted a passenger's bag from the conveyor belt when a gun inside the bag went off and barely missed the handler's leg. Kathy arrived on the scene in a matter of minutes. She worked side by side with local law-enforcement authorities because the passenger had violated a federal regulation. This, too, was part of her duty.

Kathy, a native of Atlanta, is married and the mother of a teenage son. She majored in business administration at West Georgia College before joining the ranks of the FAA.

To unwind after a busy day, she regularly bowls with a team. In the summer she and her husband, a technical representative with Xerox Corporation, swim and water ski. But a summons about a security problem at the Atlanta Airport will send her scurrying back to her office regardless of the hour. Security is her job, air safety is her mission.

Virginia Quintana Guzman, Police Detective

"I WISH I HAD STARTED THIS JOB WHEN I WAS TWENTY-one," Detective Virginia Quintana Guzman (pronounced Gooz-mon) says, her voice soft but convincing.

But how could she? At age 21, Virginia was a divorced mother of three. Lacking even a high-school diploma, Virginia was working at any job she could get—sales clerk at a bargain store, bartender, waitress. But there was never enough money to go around. Reluctantly, she added her name to the list of welfare recipients and looked forward to the day when she could repay her debt to society.

Actually Virginia's law enforcement career began much later, when she was 34. The year was 1974 and a memorable one for Brighton, Colorado, a town of 12,000 with a high ratio of Mexican-American families. Community relations in Brighton were a blight on the state, so much so that they were gaining notoriety elsewhere. Anglos and Mexican-Americans clashed daily and openly, tempers flared. Fights erupted in schools, spread to the streets and bred violence and vandalism. Every weekend, the juvenile-detention center overflowed with young people already beginning lives of crime and destruction. Then their parents became involved, and soon the community was as polarized as a basketball game—Anglos vs. Mexican-Americans.

To combat ill will and the rising tide of crime, the Brighton Police Department instituted a Community Services Bureau. Meanwhile Virginia, who is Mexican-American, had secured her high school diploma and had served in several positions that whetted her communication skills—teacher's aid at a school for migrant workers, youth adviser and a voluntary probation counselor. Timidly she applied for the job as officer in the new department, aware that her formal education and professional experience were less than impressive. But Virginia has an innate ability to inspire confidence. She was hired.

The same qualities that landed her the job set in motion a program that spelled success. Because law-enforcement officers were subjects of ridicule and scorn among the youth, Virginia organized Cops on Campus, taking officers onto junior-high campuses to talk informally with the students, to answer questions, to show that they were "just people doing their jobs."

At elementary schools, she organized Operation Brown Bag.

Virginia

While the young students ate their sandwiches and apples from paper sacks, Virginia and other officers joined them with their own bags of lunch. The officers let the students see their guns, hold their handcuffs, feel the insignia on their uniforms.

Then she set up rap sessions with troubled teenagers. Sitting in circles on schoolhouse lawns, they discussed anything from a speeding ticket to incest. For potential runaways, she arranged sessions with their families and helped them work out their problems. She secured grants to take youths from low-income families on camping trips, visits to the zoo and on picnics in the mountains.

Within a year, the tide of bitterness and violence was turned around. Tempers cooled, a spirit of tolerance and mutual concern developed, and residents of Brighton again began to show respect for one another. Now the streets are safe, and racial tension has virtually disappeared.

"I certainly didn't do it by myself," Virginia says. "I received much assistance from many people."

The program was phased out in 1977, and Virginia was transferred to the Detective Bureau. She attended the Colorado Law Enforcement Training Academy, a Crisis Intervention School and a Colorado Juvenile Conference, plus a number of training sessions and seminars. Now she handles all cases involving juveniles, sexual assault and child abuse, handling each case from the first investigation until it is resolved in court.

But her main thrust is rehabilitation. "Police work has changed in the last few years," she says. "In the past we dealt only with temporary solutions. Now we work with the perpetrator, try to get the person into counseling and change a pattern of habits. Putting people in jail isn't the answer."

At first, the 23 commissioned officers in her department looked on Virginia as a social worker. Now they come to her for advice.

Virginia, who is now enrolled in evening college and plans to get a degree, usually dresses in street clothes, always carries a gun and has at times been threatened at gunpoint.

But her greatest threat is depression. "A woman in this position must have a level head, patience, objectivity, an ability to communicate and the quality of caring," Virginia says. "She must know the community and the different cultures within the area. But she's also got to handle depression. At the end of a case, she must sit down and talk it out of her system. She just can't take it home with her."

Virginia's personal sounding board is her brother, Lieutenant Art Quintana, also with the Brighton Police Department. Art is always willing to lend his sister a sympathetic ear.

"It's very upsetting to have to go into a home and find a little child with bruises all over its body and patches of blood on its face," she says. "And having to remove a child from its home is always a trauma."

Her most traumatic moment came when, after eight years in law enforcement, she had to inform a friend and coworker, a sergeant in the Police Department, that his eight-year-old daughter had been assaulted. "That's the first time I ever really broke down and cried on the job," Virginia says.

Virginia's working hours have no beginning and no ending. "When you're dealing with people in trouble, you just don't quit at 5 o'clock," she explains. Her home phone rings almost around the clock, and she has learned to stir a pot of chili or make a bed with a telephone receiver tucked under her chin.

In 1980, Virginia was cited by the International Association of Police Chiefs and *Parade* magazine as one of the nation's top 11 policemen of the year.

As to her debt to society, any citizen of Adams County, Colorado, is willing to mark that bill *paid in full*.

Rae Hassell McNamara, State Director of Prisons

IT'S 2:00 A.M. WHEN THE JANGLING TELEPHONE JARS RAE McNamara from a deep sleep.

"It's about my brother," the voice is almost a whisper. "He's at Central Prison, you know. He says it's real cold up there at night. I got to thinking about it and worrying, and now I can't get to sleep."

The voice picks up volume as the distressed sister sheds her

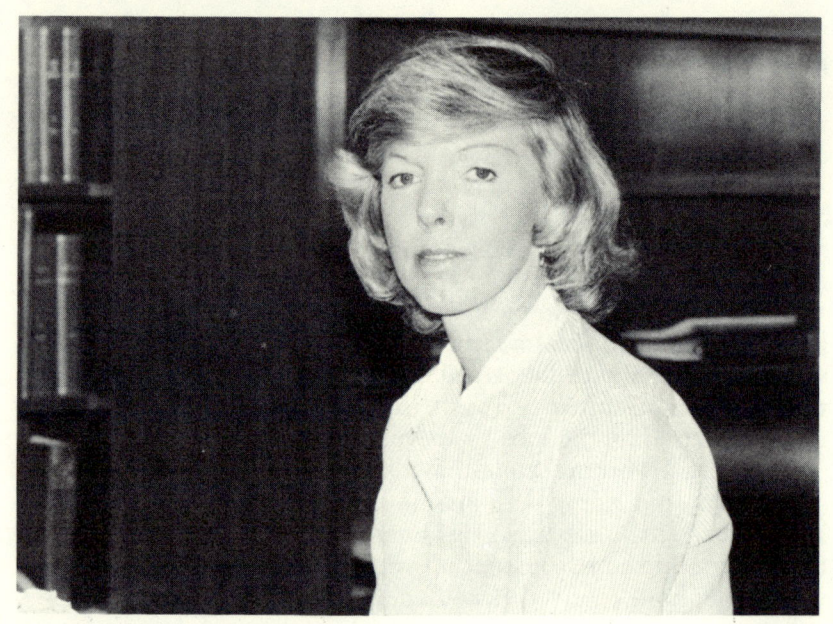

Rae

nighttime fears like an old bathrobe. Rae, her bedroom door closed so her children won't be disturbed, assures the caller she'll check into the matter. "Now try to get some sleep yourself," she adds.

The next morning, Rae arrives at her office in Raleigh, North Carolina, to face an agenda already so crowded she could use an extra two hours tacked to her day. As North Carolina Director of Prisons, she supervises an office staff of 10, plus 6,000 employees across the state. In addition, she's responsible for 16,000 prisoners.

For Rae, there's no such thing as a routine day. She may meet with a committee to plan a new building at 10:00, speak to a civic club at noon, then drive 100 miles to visit a prison unit. But a jail break or a riot or a prison fire anywhere in the state will disrupt Rae's plans and send her scurrying to the scene. Then there will be newspaper reporters and television cameras to contend with, complaints to hear, personnel problems to solve.

But Rae takes time early in the day to fulfill her nighttime promise. She orders another blanket for the brother and requests a check of the heating facilities at Central Prison.

When Rae took her oath of office in August 1981, she became the second woman in the United States to head a statewide prison system. She was 42 years old and not sure a woman could succeed in such a high-level position. All of the top members of her staff were men who had never worked for a woman, and she needed their cooperation. A major part of her job is to motivate the system's vast number of employees, to get them to try new methods, to be creative and innovative. These are the employees charged with the difficult task of actually running the individual prisons. Their jobs are depressing and sometimes thankless. Would they resist a female director?

"Now I know it makes no difference," Rae says. "The job is management. If a woman can't make it, it's because she lacks management skills, not because she's a woman."

Rae, a divorcee with two teenage children, arrived at her job "sideways, but not out of the blue." With a B.A. degree from Duke University and an M.A. in counseling from North Carolina State University, she describes her rise as a natural evolvement from 15 years of public jobs. She has been school teacher, placement director and employment counselor. In 1969, she joined the state government as a personnel analyst and interviewed employees in the Department of Corrections. In 1975, she was assigned to a legislative study commission on correctional programs. Two years later, she advanced to parole commissioner. In each job, she devoted more time than was required, excelled and was noticed. She was hired in her present job, one of the top positions in state government, by Secretary James Woodard of the Department of Corrections.

One of Rae's greatest challenges is to educate the public. "There are so many things they should know about the penal system," she says. "For instance, 70 percent of those who have served time in North Carolina prisons for the first time do not come back within three years after their release. This is encouraging, for most repeaters will probably return within a three-year period. Our citizens should know that."

And she'd like to share her abiding optimism that crime is not on the increase. The current statistics, she says, are a reflection of the "baby boom" two decades ago. "There are more people than ever before in the crime-committing age span of eighteen to twenty-four," she explains. "In a few years, the crime rate will probably diminish."

North Carolina, on the other hand, has the second-largest prison population per capita in the United States. This gives Rae little time to concentrate on other aspects, such as why less than 5 percent of the prisoners are women. "We may find answers to some interesting questions when we have time to delve further into that," she says.

Rae also finds little time to devote to her other interests —traveling, seeing shows, visiting museums and antique shops. She worked 17 straight months before taking even a weekend off.

According to Rae, the prison systems across the country need more women in top positions. "It certainly doesn't require a Ph.D.," she says. "There's no mystery or magic formula for success. It just takes good common sense. You gain competence in whatever job you're doing, you become confident, and you get noticed through good performance."

When news of Rae's appointment swept across the country, she began receiving letters from other women saying, "You've just *got* to make it for all of us."

Rae McNamara is indeed "making it."

Glossary

anesthesiologist—a physician specializing in administering sleep-producing agents
anthropology—the study of humans and relationships
backup—an out-of-sight officer or team of officers alerted to assist in need
barotrauma—injury caused by pressure in deep water
burn-out—exhaustion caused by excessive demands on energy, emotions or resources
cardiopulmonary resuscitation (CPR)—an artificial method of reviving heart and lungs
circumvention—act of anticipating, overcoming or avoiding obstacles
cocaine—a narcotic
comatose—in a state of mental or physical sluggishness
conservationist—one who advocates preserving natural resources
contraband—smuggled goods
crustaceans—certain water animals such as lobsters, shrimps, crabs, etc.
environmentalist—a person concerned with social and cultural conditions that influence the life of a community
enzyme—a complex substance produced by living cells
excrement—body waste matter
extortion—obtaining something forcibly and illegally
fecal matter—manure
felony—serious crime
forensic scientist—a scientist who deals with medical facts relating to crime or a legal problem
fugitive—someone fleeing from justice

genetic—relating to birth
hallucinate—dream or imagine while awake
heroin—a narcotic
hit man—a person paid to kill
informant—one willing to give incriminating evidence, usually to get a lighter sentence or a release from jail
key—a low island or reef
martial arts—hand-to-hand combat
mentor—a trusted and experienced counselor
mollusks—shellfish
nitrogen narcosis—bends or decompression sickness resulting from deep-water diving
no comprendo—"I do not understand" (Spanish)
oxygen toxicity—a serious condition resulting from deep-water diving
paranoid—unreasonably suspicious
parolee—an ex-prisoner who must report regularly to a parole officer
petition—a formal written request addressed to someone in power
polenta—a cornmeal mush
probation—a trial period of freedom from jail
Quāālude—an addictive drug
quantum leap—an abrupt transition
pimp—a man who solicits for a prostitute
riding shotgun—armed and on duty but not operating the vehicle
rookie—a beginner
scuba diving—diving with the use of underwater breathing apparatus
serology—a science of serums and their reactions
snorkeling—swimming underwater with a tube for breathing
staked out—set aside an area for surveillance
surveillance—close, continuous observation of a person or place
tear gas—a harmless gas that temporarily blinds the eyes with tears and is sometimes used to break up mobs
temps de fleche—a ballet step
Tudor—an English-style house marked with arches and exterior trusses
tutu—a ballet costume
under the hammer—under serious investigation
walking the scripts—writing prescriptions on stolen prescription pads

Criminal Justice Educational Opportunities

(For further information, write for catalogs at the addresses listed.)

Alabama

Alabama State University
Department of Criminal Justice
P.O. Box 271
Montgomery, Ala. 36195

Athens State College
Office of Admissions
Athens, Ala. 35611

Auburn University at Montgomery
Dept. of Justice and Public Safety
School of Sciences
Montgomery, Ala. 36193

Chattahoochee Valley Community College
Technical Arts Division
Phoenix City, Ala. 36867

George Corley Wallace State Community College
Dean of Instruction
Selma, Ala. 36701

Jacksonville State University
College of Criminal Justice
Jacksonville, Ala. 36265

Marion Military Institute
Office of Admissions
Marion, Ala. 36756

Patrick Henry State Junior College
Division of Law Enforcement
Monroeville, Ala. 36460

The University of Alabama
Dept. of Criminal Justice
Birmingham, Ala. 35294

The University of Alabama
Political Science Dept.
Huntsville, Ala. 35807

The University of Alabama
Dept. of Criminal Justice
University, Ala. 35486

Troy State University at Montgomery
Dept. of Criminal Justice
Maxwell Air Force Base, Ala. 36112

University of North Alabama
Dept. of Sociology
Florence, Ala. 35630

University of South Alabama
Dept. of Political Science
Mobile, Ala. 36688

Wallace State Community College
Law Enforcement Dept.
Hanceville, Ala. 35077

Alaska

University of Alaska at Anchorage
Justice Center
Anchorage, Alaska 99504

University of Alaska at Fairbanks
Justice Program
Fairbanks, Alaska 99701

Arizona

Arizona State University
Center of Criminal Justice
Tempe, Ariz. 85281

Arizona Western College
Financial Aid Office
Yuma, Ariz. 85364

Eastern Arizona College
Justice Administration
Thatcher, Ariz. 85552

Glendale Community College
Chair of Administration of Justice
Glendale, Ariz. 85302

Mohave Community College
Director of Administration of
  Justice
Kingman, Ariz. 86401

Northern Arizona University
Police Science and Administration
  Dept.
Flagstaff, Ariz. 86011

Pima Community College
Administration of Justice Program
Tucson, Ariz. 85709

Scottsdale Community College
Professor/Coordinator
Administration of Justice
Scottsdale, Ariz. 85253

University of Arizona
Dept. of Public Policy
Planning and Administration
Tucson, Ariz. 85721

Yavapai College
Director
AJS Education
Prescott, Ariz. 86301

Arkansas

Arkansas State University
Dept. of Sociology
Social Work and Geography
State University, Ark. 72467

Garland County Community
  College
Criminal Justice Program
Hot Springs, Ark. 71901

Mississippi County Community
  College
Division of Social and Applied
  Sciences
Blytheville, Ark. 72315

University of Arkansas at Little
  Rock
Dept. of Political Science and
  Criminal Justice
Little Rock, Ark. 72204

University of Arkansas at Pine
  Bluff
Dept. of Sociology
Pine Bluff, Ark. 71601

California

Allan Hancock College
Basic Police Academy
Santa Maria, Cal. 93454

American River College at
  Placerville
Administration of Justice
Placerville, Cal. 95667

Antelope Valley Community
  College
Dean of Technical Education
Lancaster, Cal. 93534

California Lutheran College
Administration of Justice Dept.
Thousand Oaks, Cal. 91360

California State University at
  Fresno
Dept. of Criminology
Fresno, Cal. 93740

California State University at
  Fullerton
Criminal Justice Dept.
Fullerton, Cal. 93634

California State University at Long
  Beach
Dept. of Criminal Justice
Long Beach, Cal. 90840

California State University at
  Sacramento
Dept. of Criminal Justice and
  Forensic Science
Sacramento, Cal. 95819

California State College at San Bernardino
Criminal Justice Program
San Bernardino, Cal. 92407

Cerritos College
Administration of Justice Dept.
Norwalk, Cal. 90650

Chaffey Community College
Administration of Justice
Alta Loma, Cal. 91701

Chapman College
Criminal Justice Dept.
Orange, Cal. 92666

Claremont Graduate School
Dept. of Criminal Science
Claremont, Cal. 91711

College of Marin
Administration of Justice
Kentfield, Cal. 94904

College of San Mateo
Administration of Justice
San Mateo, Cal. 94402

College of the Sequoias
Criminal Justice Dept.
Visalia, Cal. 93277

College of the Siskiyous
Administration of Justice Coordinator
Weed, Cal. 96904

Cuenta College
P.O. Box J
San Luis Obispo, Cal. 93406

El Camino Community College
Administration of Justice
Torrance, Cal. 90505

Fullerton College
Chairman of Police Science Dept.
Fullerton, Cal. 92634

Gavilan College
Administration of Justice
Gilroy, Cal. 95020

Glendale Community College
Glendale, Cal. 91206

Golden West College
Criminal Justice Training Center
Huntington Beach, Cal. 92647

John F. Kennedy University
School of Management
Orinda, Cal. 94563

Lassen College
Student Services Office
Susanville, Cal. 96130

Long Beach City College
Dean of Financial Aid
Long Beach, Cal. 90808

Los Angeles City College
Law Department
Los Angeles, Cal. 90025

Mendocino Community College
Administration of Justice Dept.
Ukiah, Cal. 45482

Merced College
Administration of Justice Program
Merced, Cal. 95340

Mount San Antonio College
Dept. of Public Service
Walnut, Cal. 91789

Mt. San Jacinto College
Dean of Vocational Instruction
San Jacinto, Cal. 92383-2399

Napa College
Coordinator of Criminal Justice
Napa, Cal. 94558

National University
Criminal Justice Dept.
San Diego, Cal. 92108

Ohlone College
Admissions Dept.
Fremont, Cal. 94538

Palomar Community College
Dean of Vocational Education
San Marcos, Cal. 92069

Pasadena City College
Administration of Justice
Pasadena, Cal. 91106

Rio Hondo College
Public Service Dept.
Whittier, Cal. 90608

Riverside City College
Administration of Justice
Riverside, Cal. 92506

Sacramento City College
3835 Freeport Blvd.
Sacramento, Cal. 95823

San Jose State University
Administration of Justice Dept.
San Jose, Cal. 95192

Santa Barbara City College
721 Cliff Drive
Santa Barbara, Cal. 93109

Sierra Community College
Dept. of Social Sciences
Rocklin, Cal. 95677

Southwestern College
Office of Admissions and Records
Chula Vista, Cal. 92010

University of California at Berkeley
School of Law
Berkeley, Cal. 94720

University of California at Irvine
Program in Social Ecology
Irvine, Cal. 92717

University of Redlands
Program Development
Redlands, Cal. 92373

University of Southern California
Judicial Administration Program
Los Angeles, Cal. 90007

West Valley College
Administration of Justice Dept.
Saratoga, Cal. 95070

Yuba Community College
Administration of Justice Dept.
Marysville, Cal. 95901

Canada

Algonquin College of Applied
  Arts and Technology
Coordinator of Law and Security
  Program
Ottawa, Ontario, Canada
  K2G 1VB

Douglas College
The Admissions Officer
New Westminster, British
  Columbia, Canada V3L 5B2

Humber College of Applied Arts
  and Technology
Program Coordinator
Rexdale, Ontario, Canada
  M9W 5L7

Lethbridge Community College
Law Enforcement Program
Lethbridge, Alberta, Canada
  T1K 1L6

Mount Royal College
Justice Administration Dept.
Calgary, Alberta, Canada
  T3E 6K6

University of Ottawa
Dept. of Criminology
Ottawa, Ontario, Canada
  K1N 6N5

Colorado

Arapahoe Community College
Administration of Justice
Littleton, Colo. 80120

Mesa College
Law Enforcement Program
Grand Junction, Colo. 81501

Metropolitan State College
Dept. of Criminal Justice and
  Criminology
Denver, Colo. 80204

Pikes Peak Community College
Criminal Justice Program
Colorado Springs, Colo. 80906

Trinidad State Junior College
Law Enforcement Dept.
Trinidad, Colo. 81082

University of Colorado
Director of Criminal Justice
  Programs
Denver, Colo. 80203

University of Colorado at Denver
Criminal Justice Division
Denver, Colo. 80202

University of Denver College of
  Law
Director of Special Programs
Denver, Colo. 80204

Connecticut

Eastern Connecticut State College
Sociology Dept.
Willimantic, Conn. 86226

Housatonic Community College
Director of Admissions
Bridgeport, Conn. 06608

Mattatuck Community College
Criminal Justice Program
Waterbury, Conn. 06708

Northwestern Connecticut
  Community College
Dean of Instruction
Winsted, Conn. 06098

Sacred Heart University
Criminal Justice Program
Bridgeport, Conn. 06606

Tunxis Community College
Director of Admissions
Farmington, Conn. 06032

University of New Haven
Division of Criminal Justice
West Haven, Conn. 06516

Delaware

Delaware Technical and
  Community College
Criminal Justice Dept.
Georgetown, Dela. 19947

Delaware Technical and
  Community College
Criminal Justice
Newark, Dela. 19702

University of Delaware
Division of Criminal Justice
Newark, Dela. 19711

District of Columbia

The American University
School of Justice
Washington, D.C. 20016

Florida

Broward Community College
Criminal Justice Institute
Fort Lauderdale, Fla. 33314

Chipola Community College
Coordinator of Law Enforcement
Marianna, Fla. 32466

Clearwater Christian College
Admissions Office
Clearwater, Fla. 33519

Daytona Beach Community
  College
Public Services Dept.
Daytona Beach, Fla. 32015

Edison Community College
Division of Applied Sciences
Fort Myers, Fla. 33907

Florida Atlantic University
Criminal Justice Program
Boca Raton, Fla. 33431

Florida International University
Criminal Justice Dept.
Miami, Fla. 33181

Florida Junior College at
  Jacksonville
Director of Criminal Justice
Jacksonville, Fla. 32216

Florida Keys Community College
Florida Keys Institute of Criminal
  Justice
Key West, Fla. 33040

Florida State University
School of Criminology
Tallahassee, Fla. 32306

Indian River Community College
Police Academy Coordinator
Fort Pierce, Fla. 33450

Lake City Community College
Police Science and Corrections
Lake City, Fla. 32055

Miami-Dade Community College
Administration of Criminal Justice
  Program
Miami, Fla. 33167

Okaloosa-Walton Junior College
Admissions
Niceville, Fla. 32578

Palm Beach Junior College
Criminal Justice Dept.
Lake Worth, Fla. 33461

Pasco-Hernando Community
  College
Law Enforcement Programs
Dade City, Fla. 33525

Pensacola Junior College
Public Service Careers
Pensacola, Fla. 32504

Rollins College
Criminal Justice Program
Winter Park, Fla. 32789

St. Johns River Community
  College
Dept. of Law Enforcement
Palatka, Fla. 32077

St. Petersburg Junior College
Police Administration
St. Petersburg, Fla. 33733

Sante Fe Community College
Public Safety Program
Gainesville, Fla. 32601

South Florida Junior College
Vocational-Technical Division
Avon Park, Fla. 33825

Tallahassee Community College
Criminal Justice Dept.
Tallahassee, Fla. 32304

University of Central Florida
Dept. of Public Service
   Administration
Orlando, Fla. 32816

University of Tampa
Social Science Dept.
Tampa, Fla. 33606

University of West Florida
Criminal Justice Program
Pensacola, Fla. 32504

Valencia Community College
P.O. Box 3028
Orlando, Fla. 32822

Georgia

Albany Junior College
Director of Criminal Justice
Albany, Ga. 31707

Armstrong State College
Department of Criminal Justice
Savannah, Ga. 31406

Atlanta University
Criminal Justice Institute
Atlanta, Ga. 30314

Augusta College
Criminal Justice Program
Augusta, Ga. 30910

Bainbridge Junior College
Division of Social Science
Bainbridge, Ga. 31717

Clayton Junior College
P.O. Box 285
Morrow, Ga. 30260

Columbus College
Criminal Justice Dept
Columbus, Ga. 31907

Dalton Junior College
Criminal Justice Program
Dalton, Ga. 30720

Dekalb Community College
Admissions Office
Clarkston, Ga. 30021

Gainesville Junior College
Social Sciences Division
Gainesville, Ga. 30501

Georgia State University
Criminal Justice Program
Atlanta, Ga. 30303

Mercer University
Dept. of Sociology and
   Criminology
Macon, Ga. 31207

South Georgia College
Criminal Justice Program
Douglas, Ga. 31533

University of Georgia
Criminal Justice Studies Program
Athens, Ga. 30602

Valdosta State College
Coordinator of Criminal Justice
Valdosta, Ga. 31601

Hawaii

Chaminade University
Criminal Justice Dept.
Honolulu, Hawaii 96816

Hawaii Community College of the
   University of Hawaii at Hilo
Admissions Officer
University of Hawaii at Hilo
Hilo, Hawaii 96720

Maui Community College
Police Science
Kahului, Maui, Hawaii 96732

Idaho

Ricks College
Dept. of Sociology and Law
   Enforcement
Rexburg, Idaho 83440

School of Vocational-Technical
 Education
Idaho State University
Law Enforcement Program
Pocatello, Idaho 83209

Illinois

Aurora College
Criminal Justice Dept.
Aurora, Ill. 60507

Black Hawk College
East Campus
Kewanee, Ill. 61443

Bradley University
Administration of Criminal Justice
 Program
Peoria, Ill. 61625

Carl Sandburg College
Admissions Office
Galesburg, Ill. 61401

Highland Community College
Humanities/Social Science
 Division
Freeport, Ill. 61032

Illinois Central College
Community/Environmental
 Studies
East Peoria, Ill. 61635

Illinois State University
Criminal Justice Sciences
Normal, Ill. 61761

Illinois Valley Community College
Criminal Justice
Oglesby, Ill. 61340

Kankakee Community College
Law Enforcement Program
Kankakee, Ill. 60901

Kishwaukee College
Ind. Tech./Public Service
 Occupations Division
Malta, Ill. 60150

Lincoln College
Criminal Justice Program
Lincoln, Ill. 62656

Lincoln Land Community College
Social and Criminal Justice Dept.
Springfield, Ill. 62708

Loyola University of Chicago
Criminal Justice Dept.
Chicago, Ill. 60611

MacMurray College
Program in Administration of
 Justice
Jacksonville, Ill. 62650

Moraine Valley Community
 College
Behavioral Sciences and Public
 Services Program
Palos Hills, Ill. 60465

Oakton Community College
Law Enforcement Curriculum
Des Plaines, Ill. 60016

Olivet Nazarene College
Box 123
Kankakee, Ill. 60901

Parkland College
Coordinator/Law Enforcement
Champaign, Ill. 61820

Quad Cities Training Center
Black Hawk College
Director
East Moline, Ill. 61244

Sangamon State University
Director/Social Justice Professions
 Program
Springfield, Ill. 62708

Sauk Valley College
Criminal Justice Program
Dixon, Ill. 61021

Southern Illinois University at
 Carbondale
Administration of Justice
Carbondale, Ill. 62901

University of Illinois at Chicago
 Circle
Director of Undergraduate Studies
Chicago, Ill. 60680

Western Illinois University
Dept. of Law Enforcement
Macomb, Ill. 61455

William Rainey Harper College
Coordinator/Criminal Justice
 Program
Palatine, Ill. 60067

Indiana

Ball State University
Dept. of Criminal Justice and
 Corrections
Muncie, Ind. 47306

Indiana Central University
Director/Criminal Justice
  Programs
Indianapolis, Ind. 46227

Indiana State University
Criminology Dept.
Terra Haute, Ind. 57809

Indiana University East
Public and Environmental Affairs
Richmond, Ind. 47374

Indiana University-Purdue
  University
Criminal Justice Program
Fort Wayne, Ind. 46805

Marion College
Director of Criminal Justice
  Education
Marion, Ind. 46952

University of Evansville
Director of Criminal Justice
  Program
Evansville, Ind. 47702

Vincennes University
Coordinator of Law Enforcement
  Program
Vincennes, Ind. 47591

Iowa

Des Moines Area Community
  College
Criminal Justice Dept.
Ankeny, Iowa 50021

Hawkeye Institute of Technology
Criminal Justice/Public Services
  Dept.
Waterloo, Iowa 50704

Indian Hills Community College
Criminal Justice Dept.
Ottumwa, Iowa 52501

Iowa Central Community College
Admissions
Fort Dodge, Iowa 50501

Iowa Wesleyan College
Dean of Admissions
Mt. Pleasant, Iowa 52641

Kirkwood Community College
Public Safety Program
Cedar Rapids, Iowa 52406

Morningside College
Criminal Justice Program
Sioux City, Iowa 51106

Southwestern Community College
Law Enforcement Instructor
Creston, Iowa 50801

The University of Iowa
Admissions Committee
Iowa City, Iowa 52242

Waldorf College
Director of Admissions
Forest City, Iowa 50436

Wartburg College
Dept. of Admissions
Waverly, Iowa 50677

Kansas

Butler County Community College
Director of Continuing Education
El Dorado, Kan. 67042

Colby Community College
Dean of Instruction
Colby, Kan. 67701

Cowley County Community
  College and Vocational-
  Technical School
Director
Arkansas City, Kansas 67005

Highland Community College
Dean of Student Affairs
Highland, Kan. 66035

Hutchinson Community College
Director of Admissions
Hutchinson, Kan. 67501

Johnson County Community
  College
Administration of Justice Program
Overland Park, Kan. 66210

Kansas City, Kansas, Community
  College
Law Enforcement Education
  Program
Kansas City, Kan. 66112

Kansas Wesleyan
Administration of Justice Program
Salina, Kan. 67401

Labette Community College
Director/Criminal Justice Dept.
Parsons, Kan. 67357

St. Mary of the Plains College
Criminal Justice Dept.
Dodge City, Kan. 67801

Washburn University of Topeka
Dept. of Criminal Justice
Topeka, Kan. 66621

Wichita State University
Dept. of Administration of Justice
Wichita, Kan. 67208

Kentucky

Campbellsville College
Director of Admissions
Campbellsville, Ky. 42718

Eastern Kentucky University
College of Law Enforcement
Richmond, Ky. 40475

Hopkinsville Community College
Coordinator/Law Enforcement
Hopkinsville, Ky. 42240

Kentucky State University
Coordinator/Criminal Justice
Frankfort, Ky. 40601

Kentucky Wesleyan College
Dept. of Behavioral Sciences
Owensboro, Ky. 42301

Morehead State University
Dept. of Sociology,
 Social Work and Corrections
Morehead, Ky. 40351

Murray State University
Director/Division of Criminal
 Justice
Murray, Ky. 42071

University of Louisville
School of Justice Administration
Louisville, Ky. 40292

Louisiana

Bossier Parish Community College
2719 Airline Drive N.
Bossier City, La. 71111

Grambling State University
Dept. of Criminal Justice
Grambling, La. 71245

Louisiana State University at Baton
 Rouge
Dept. of Criminal Justice
106 David Boyd Hall
Baton Rouge, La. 70803

Louisiana State University at
 Eunice
Div. of Liberal Arts
P.O. Box 1129
Eunice, La. 70535

Louisiana State University at
 Shreveport
Criminal Justice Dept.
8515 Youree Drive
Shreveport, La. 71115

Loyola University
Studies in Criminal Justice
Box 55
New Orleans, La. 70118

McNeese State University
Dept. of Social Sciences
Lake Charles, La. 70601

Nicholls State University
Government and Criminal Justice
Box 2024
Thibodaux, La. 70301

Northeast Louisiana University
Criminal Justice Program
Monroe, La. 71209

Southeastern Louisiana University
Criminal Justice Dept.
Hammond, La. 70402

University of Southwestern
 Louisiana
Criminal Justice Program
Box 41652
Lafayette, La. 70504

Maine

Southern Maine Vocational-
 Technical Institute
Law Enforcement Technology
 Dept.
Fort Road
South Portland, Maine 04106

University of Maine at Presque Isle
Criminal Justice Program
181 Main St.
Presque Isle, Maine 04769

Maryland

Allegany Community College
Criminal Justice Program
Cumberland, Md. 21502

Anne Arundel Community
 College
Law Enforcement Dept.
101 College Parkway
Arnold, Md. 21012

Catonsville Community College
Criminal Justice Program
Catonsville, Md. 21228

Chesapeake College
Director of Admissions
Wye Mills, Md. 21679

Community College of Baltimore
Dept. of Administration of
 Justice and Public Safety
Lombard and Market Place
Baltimore, Md. 21202

Frederick Community College
Social Science Dept.
7932 Oppossumtown Pike
Frederick, Md. 21701

Hagerstown Junior College
Registrar
751 Robinwood Drive
Hagerstown, Md. 21740

Maryland Institute of Criminal
 Justice
Suite 303
Severna Park, Md. 21146

Montgomery College
Criminal Justice Program
Rockville, Md. 20850

Prince George's Community
 College
301 Largo Road
Largo, Md. 20870

University of Baltimore
Institute of Criminal Justice and
 Criminology
College Park, Md. 20742

Massachusetts

American International College
Criminal Justice Studies
Box 15-L
Springfield, Mass. 01109

Boston State College
Public Service Dept.
Boston, Mass. 02115

Bristol Community College
Director of Criminal Justice
 Program
777 Elsbree St.
Fall River, Mass. 02720

Clark University
Dept. of Sociology
Worcester, Mass. 01610

Dean Junior College
Director of Admissions
99 Main St.
Franklin, Mass. 02038

Middlesex Community College
Law Enforcement/Security
 Administration Dept.
Springs Road (Box T)
Bedford, Mass. 01730

Northeastern University
College of Criminal Justice
144 KV
Boston, Mass. 02115

Northern Essex Community
 College
Criminal Justice
100 Elliott St.
Haverhill, Mass. 01830

Quincy Junior College
34 Coddington St.
Quincy, Mass. 02169

Stonehill College
Dean of Admissions
North Easton, Mass. 02356

Suffolk University
Dept. of Sociology
Boston, Mass. 02114

University of Lowell
Administration of Law and Justice
Kitson Hall-214
Lowell, Mass. 01854

Westfield State College
Criminal Justice Dept.
Western Ave.
Westfield, Mass. 01086

Michigan

Adrian College
Criminal Justice Program
Jones Hall
Adrian, Mich. 49221

Criminal Justice Educational Opportunities

Alpena Community College
Law Enforcement Education
Alpena, Mich. 49707

Delta College
Law Enforcement Curriculum
University Center, Mich. 48710

Eastern Michigan University
Criminal Justice and Criminology
Ypsilanti, Mich. 48197

Gogebic Community College
Greenbush and Jackson Roads
Ironwood, Mich. 49938

Grand Rapids Junior College
Criminal Justice Dept. or Law
 Enforcement Program
143 Bostwick NE
Grand Rapids, Mich. 49502

Jackson Community College
Criminal Justice Programs
2111 Emmons Road
Jackson, Mich. 49201

Kalamazoo Valley Community
 College
Regional Police Training Academy
 and Criminal Justice Programs
6767 West O Ave.
Kalamazoo, Mich. 49009

Kellogg Community College
Criminal Justice Education
450 North Ave.
Battle Creek, Mich. 49016

Lake Michigan College
Criminal Justice and Public Safety
 Programs
2755 East Napier Ave.
Benton Harbor, Mich. 49022

Lake Superior State College
Criminal Justice Program
Sault Ste. Marie, Mich. 49783

Madonna College
Criminal Justice Dept.
36600 Schoolcraft Road
Livonia, Mich. 48150

Mercy College of Detroit
Center for Administration of
 Justice
8200 West Outer Drive
Detroit, Mich. 48219

Michigan State University
School of Criminal Justice
560 Baker Hall
East Lansing, Mich. 48824

Mid Michigan Community College
Occupational Education
1375 S. Clare Ave.
Harrison, Mich. 48625

Muskegon Community College
221 S. Quarterline
Muskegon, Mich. 49442

Nazareth College
Nazareth, Mich. 49074

Northern Michigan University
Criminal Justice Dept.
111 Pierce Hall
Marquette, Mich. 49855

Northwestern Michigan College
1701 E. Front St.
Traverse City, Mich. 49684

Oakland University
Social Justice and Corrections
 Programs
520 Varuer Hall
Rochester, Mich. 48063

St. Clair County Community
 College
Criminal Justice Education
323 Erie St.
Port Huron, Mich. 48060

Suomi College
Criminal Justice Dept.
Hancock, Mich. 49930

University of Detroit
Criminal Justice
4001 W. McNichols
Detroit, Mich. 48221

University of Michigan at Flint
Dept. of Sociology
Flint, Mich. 48503

Washtenaw Community College
Public Service Careers
4800 E. Huron River Drive
Ann Arbor, Mich. 48106

Wayne State University
Criminal Justice Dept.
6001 Cass. Room 214
Detroit, Mich. 48202

Western Michigan University
Dept. of Sociology
Criminal Justice Program
Kalamazoo, Mich. 49008

Minnesota

Bemidji State University
Criminal Justice Program
Bemidji, Minn. 56601

College of St. Thomas
Dept. of Sociology
2115 Summit Ave., or
 Criminal Justice Program
Box 4112
St. Paul, Minn. 55105

Golden Valley Lutheran College
Law Enforcement Program
6125 Olson Memorial Highway
Golden Valley, Minn. 55422

Mankato State University
Law Enforcement Program
Box 007
Mankato, Minn. 56001

Normandale Community College
Law Enforcement Dept.
9300 France Ave. S.
Bloomington, Minn. 55431

St. Cloud State University
Center for Studies in Criminal
 Justice
St. Cloud, Minn. 56301

University of Minnesota at Duluth
Center for Criminal Justice Studies
Dept. of Sociology/Anthropology
Duluth, Minn. 55812

Willmar Community College
Willmar, Minn. 56201

Winona State University
Dept. of Sociology
Minne Hall
Winona, Minn. 55987

Mississippi

Copiah-Lincoln Junior College
Dept. of Law Enforcement
Natchez Campus
Natchez, Miss. 39120

Mississippi Gulf Coast Junior
 College
Law Enforcement and Technical
 Programs
Jefferson Davis Campus
Gulfport, Miss. 39501

Mississippi State University
Dept. of Social Work
Corrections Sequence
P.O. Drawer HU
Mississippi State, Miss. 39762

Mississippi Valley State University
Criminal Justice Program
Box 123
Itta Bena, Miss. 38941

North East Mississippi Junior
 College
Director of Law Enforcement
Booneville, Miss. 38829

Northwest Mississippi Junior
 College
Law Enforcement Dept.
Senatobia, Miss. 38668

University of Mississippi
Law Enforcement Programs
University, Miss. 38677

University of Southern Mississippi
Criminal Justice Dept.
Hattiesburg, Miss. 39401

Missouri

Central Missouri State University
Criminal Justice Administration
 Dept.
313 Humphreys Bldg.
Warrensburg, Mo. 64093

Drury College
Criminal Justice
Dept. of Behavioral Science
Springfield, Mo. 65802

Evangel College
Behavioral Sciences
111 N. Glentstone
Springfield, Mo. 65802

Lincoln University
Criminal Justice Program
Box 215
Jefferson City, Mo. 65101

Longview Community College
Correctional Services / Human
  Services Programs, or
  Law Enforcement Program /
  Police Training Seminars
Lee's Summit, Mo. 64063

Missouri Southern State College
Criminal Justice Programs
Police Academy Bldg.
Newman and Duquesne Rds.
Joplin, Mo. 64801

Missouri Western State College
Dept. of Criminal Justice
4525 Downs Drive
St. Joseph, Mo. 64507

Northeast Missouri State University
Criminal Justice Program
Kirksville, Mo. 63501

Penn Valley Community College
Administration of Justice Dept.
3201 Southwest Trafficway
Kansas City, Mo. 64111

Rockhurst College
5225 Troast
Kansas City, Mo. 64110

St. Louis Community College at
  Forest Park
Criminal Justice Dept.
5600 Oakland Ave.
St. Louis, Mo. 63110

St. Louis Community College at
  Meramec
11333 Big Bend Blvd.
St. Louis, Mo. 63122

St. Louis University
Metropolitan College
221 N. Grand
St. Louis, Mo. 63103

St. Mary's College of O'Fallon
200 N. Main St.
O'Fallon, Mo. 63366

School of the Ozarks
Dept. of Criminal Justice
Point Lookout, Mo. 65726

Southeast Missouri State University
Dept. of Criminal Justice
Cape Giradeau, Mo. 63701

State Fair Community College
Law Enforcement
Sedalia, Mo. 65301

University of Missouri at Kansas
  City
Administration of Justice Dept.
Kansas City, Mo. 64110

University of Missouri at St. Louis
Dept. of Administration of Justice
8001 Natural Bridge Road
St. Louis, Mo. 63121

Montana

Montana State University
Social Justice Program
Wilson Hall
Bozeman, Montana, 59715

University of Montana
Dept. of Sociology
Missoula, Montana 59812

Nebraska

Chadron State College
Criminal Justice Dept.
Chadron, Neb. 69337

Kearney State College
Criminal Justice Program
Kearney, Neb. 68847

Metropolitan Technical
  Community College
South Omaha Campus
P.O. Box 3777
Omaha, Neb. 68137

Mid Plains Community College
Criminal Justice
McDonald Belton Campus
North Platte, Neb. 69101

Nebraska Western College
Criminal Justice Dept.
Scottsbluff, Neb. 69361

Northeast Technical Community
  College
Dept. of Criminal Justice
801 E. Benjamin Ave.
Norfolk, Neb. 68701

University of Nebraska at Omaha
Criminal Justice Dept.
1100 Neihardt Complex
540 North 16th
Lincoln, Neb. 68588,
  or Criminal Justice Dept.
Annex 26
60th and Dodge Sts.
Omaha, Neb. 68182

Nevada

Clark County Community College
Administration of Justice
3200 E. Cheyenne Ave.
N. Las Vegas, Nevada 89030

University of Nevada at Las Vegas
Criminal Justice Dept.
4505 Maryland Parkway S.
Las Vegas, Nevada 89154

University of Nevada at Reno
Dept. of Criminal Justice
Reno, Nevada 89557

New Hampshire

Saint Anselm's College
Criminal Justice Programs
Manchester, N.H. 03102

New Jersey

Atlantic Community College
Public Safety Programs
Mays Landing, N.J. 08330

Burlington County College
Criminal Justice Program
Pemberton-Browns Mills Rd.
Pemberton, N.J. 08068

Camden County College
Public Safety and Administration
   Programs
Blackwood, N.J. 08012

County College of Morris
Criminal Justice Dept.
   AS/C 311
Route 10 and Center Grove Rd.
Randolph Township, N.J. 07869

Glassboro State College
Law/Justice Dept.
Glassboro, N.J. 08028

Kean College
Criminal Justice/Political Science
   Dept.
Union, N.J. 07083

Mercer County Community
   College
Div. of Humanities
P.O. Box "B"
1200 Old Trenton Rd.
Trenton, N.J. 08690

Ocean County College
Criminal Justice Program
College Dr.
Toms River, N.J. 08753

Richard Stockton State College
Criminal Justice Program
Pomona, N.J. 08240

Rutgers, the State University of
   New Jersey
School of Criminal Justice
15 Washington St.
Newark, N.J. 07102

Seton Hall University
Dept. of Sociology/
   Anthropology/Criminal
   Justice
South Orange Ave.
South Orange, N.J. 07079

Somerset County College
P.O. Box 3300
Somerville, N.J. 08876

Trenton State College
Dept. of Criminal Justice
P.O. Box 940
Trenton, N.J. 08625

Union College
Dept. of Criminal Justice
1033 Springfield Ave.
Cranford, N.J. 07016

New Mexico

Eastern New Mexico University at
   Clovis
Criminal Justice Program
Schepps Blvd.
Clovis, New Mexico 88101

New Mexico Military Institute
Dept. of Law Enforcement
Roswell, New Mexico 88201

New Mexico State University at
   Carlsbad
1500 University Dr.
Carlsbad, New Mexico 88220

New Mexico State University at Las
   Cruces
Dept. of Police Science
Box 3487
Las Cruces, New Mexico 88003

Western New Mexico University
Office of Criminal Justice
College Ave.
Silver City, New Mexico 88061

New York

Adirondack Community College
Criminal Justice
Glens Falls, N.Y. 12801

Alfred University
Div. of Social Sciences
Box 545
Alfred, N.Y. 14802

Broome Community College
Criminal Justice
Binghamton, N.Y. 13905

Canton Agriculture and Technical
   College
Criminal Justice Program
Canton, N.Y. 13617

Columbia-Greene Community
   College
Criminal Justice Dept.
P.O. Box 1000
Hudson, N.Y. 12534

Dutchess Community College
Criminal Justice Program
Poughkeepsie, N.Y. 12601

D'Youville College
Sociology/Criminal Justice
320 Porter Ave.
Buffalo, N.Y. 14201

Elmira College
Criminal Justice Program
Elmira, N.Y. 14901

Erie Community College North
Criminal Justice Curriculum
Main and Youngs Rd.
Buffalo, N.Y. 14221

Erie Community College/North
   Campus
Criminal Justice Dept.
Main and Youngs Rd.
Williamsville, N.Y. 14221

Fulton-Montgomery Community
   College
Career Education
Johnstown, N.Y. 12095

Herkimer County Community
   College
Herkimer, N.Y. 13350

Hudson Valley Community
   College
Criminal Justice Dept.
80 Vandenburgh Ave.
Troy, N.Y. 12180

Iona College
Criminal Justice Dept.
715 North Ave.
New Rochelle, N.Y. 10801

Jamestown Community College
Public Safety Program
Jamestown, N.Y. 14701

Jefferson Community College
Watertown, N.Y. 13601

Jersey City State College
Dept. of Criminal Justice
2039 Kennedy Blvd.
Jersey City, N.J. 07305

John Jay College of Criminal
   Justice
City University of N.Y.
445 W. 59 St.
New York, N.Y. 10019

Long Island University
Criminal Justice Dept.
Brooklyn, N.Y. 11201

Long Island University/C.W. Post
   Center
Dept. of Criminal Justice
Greenvale, N.Y. 11548

Mater Dei College
Riverside Drive
Ogdensburg, N.Y. 13669

Mercy College
Dept. of Criminal Justice and
   Public Safety
Dobbs Ferry, N.Y. 10522

Mohawk Valley Community
   College
Criminal Justice
1101 Sherman Dr.
Utica, N.Y. 13501

Monroe Community College
Criminal Justice Dept.
1000 East Henrietta Rd.
Rochester, N.Y. 14623

Nassau Community College
Criminal Justice Dept.
Stewart Ave.
Garden City, N.Y. 11530

New York Institute of Technology
Criminal Justice Program
P.O. Box 170
Wheatley Road
Old Westbury, N.Y. 11568

Orange County Community
College
Social and Behavioral Sciences Div.
Middletown, N.Y. 10940

Pace University
Criminal Justice Program
Pleasantville, N.Y. 10570

Rochester Institute of Technology
Criminal Justice Dept.
One Lomb Memorial Dr.
Rochester, N.Y. 14623

Rockland Community College
Criminal Justice Dept.
145 College Rd.
Suffern, N.Y. 10901

Russell Sage College
Criminal Science Dept.
Troy, N.Y. 12180

St. John's University
Grand Central at Utopia Parkways
Jamaica, N.Y. 11439

St. Thomas Aquinas College
Criminal Justice
Rt. 340
Sparkhill, N.Y. 10976

Schenectady County Community
College
Dept. of Business and Law
Washington Ave.
Schenectady, N.Y. 12305

State University Agriculture and
Technical College
Criminal Justice Dept.
Melville Rd.
Farmingdale, N.Y. 11735

State University College at Buffalo
Criminal Justice Dept.
1300 Elmwood Ave.
Buffalo, N.Y. 14222

State University College at
Fredonia
Coordinator of Law and Justice
Fredonia, N.Y. 14063

State University of New York at
Albany
School of Criminal Justice
135 Western Ave.
Albany, N.Y. 12222

State University of New York
College at Brockport
Criminal Justice Dept.
135 Hartwell Hall
Brockport, N.Y. 14420

State University of New York
College of Technology
Criminal Justice
811 Court St.
Utica, N.Y. 13502

Suffolk County Community
College
Criminal Justice Dept.
Seldon, N.Y. 11784

Ulster County Community College
Criminal Justice Dept.
Stone Ridge, N.Y. 12484

Westchester Community College
Criminal Justice
75 Grasslands Rd.
Valhalla, N.Y. 10595

North Carolina

Appalachian State University
Political Science/Criminal Justice
Boone, N.C. 28608

Asheville-Buncombe Technical
College
Dept. of Criminal Justice
340 Victoria Rd.
Asheville, N.C. 28801

Cape Fear Technical Institute
Criminal Justice Dept.
411 N. Front St.
Wilmington, N.C. 28401

Cleveland County Technical
College
Criminal Justice Dept.
137 S. Post Rd.
Shelby, N.C. 28150

Criminal Justice Educational Opportunities

Coastal Carolina Community
  College
4444 Western Blvd.
Jacksonville, N.C. 28540

Craven Community College
Criminal Justice
P.O. Box 885
New Bern, N.C. 28560

East Carolina University
Correctional Services
Greenville, N.C. 27834

Edgecombe Technical College
Box 2307
Tarboro, N.C. 27886

Fayetteville Technical Institute
Criminal Justice
P.O. Box 35236
Fayetteville, N.C. 28304

Forsyth Technical Institute
Police Science Dept.
2100 Silas Creek Parkway
Winston-Salem, N.C. 27103

Gaston College
Dept. of Criminal Justice
Dallas, N.C. 28034

Guilford College
Administration of Justice
5800 W. Friendly Ave.
Greensboro, N.C. 27408

Halifax Community College
Criminal Justice Dept.
P.O. Drawer 809
Weldon, N.C. 27890

Haywood Technical College
Freedlander Dr.
Clyde, N.C. 28721

James Sprunt Technical College
Criminal Justice Technology Dept.
P.O. Box 398
Kenansville, N.C. 28349

North Carolina State University
Dept. of Political Science
  B-11-M Nelson Hall,
or Dept. of Sociology
  318-1911 Bldg.
Raleigh, N.C. 27650

North Carolina Wesleyan College
Criminal Justice Dept.
Wesleyan Station
Rocky Mount, N.C. 27801

Pembroke State University
Dept. of Sociology
Pembroke, N.C. 28372

Pfeiffer College
Dept. of Criminal Justice
P.O. Box 56
Misenheimer, N.C. 28109

Pitt Community College
P.O. Box 7007
Greenville, N.C. 27834

Richmond Technical College
Criminal Justice
P.O. Box 1189
Hamlet, N.C. 28345

Rowan Technical College
Criminal Justice Program
1595 Klumac Rd.
Salisbury, N.C. 28144

Sacred Heart College
Criminal Justice Dept.
Belmont, N.C. 28012

Shaw University/Fayetteville
  Campus
Criminal Justice Dept.
2215 Murchison Rd.
Fayetteville, N.C. 28301

Southwestern Technical College
P.O. Box 67
Sylva, N.C. 28779

Surry Community College
Criminal Justice Dept.
Dobson, N.C. 27017

Tri-County Community College
Police Science Dept.
P.O. Box 40
Murphy, N.C. 28906

University of North Carolina at
  Charlotte
Dept. of Criminal Justice
UNCC Station
Charlotte, N.C. 28223

University of North Carolina at
  Wilmington
Dept. of Sociology and
  Anthropology
Wilmington, N.C. 28403

Vance-Granville Community
  College
P.O. Box 917
Henderson, N.C. 27536

Wake Technical College
Police Science Technology
9101 Fayetteville Rd.
Raleigh, N.C. 27603

Wayne Community College
Caller Box 8002
Goldsboro, N.C. 27530

Western Carolina University
Criminal Justice Program
208A Belk
Cullowhee, N.C. 28723

Wilkes Community College
Dept. of Human Services
Drawer 120
Wilkesboro, N.C. 28697

Wilson County Technical Institute
Criminal Justice Technology
902 Herring Ave.
Wilson, N.C. 27893

North Dakota

Bismarck Junior College
Criminal Justice Dept.
Bismarck, N. Dak. 58501

Minot State College
Dept. of Criminal Justice
Box 143
Minot, N. Dak. 58701

University of North Dakota
Criminal Justice Studies
Dept. of Political Science
Grand Forks, N. Dak. 58202

Ohio

Baldwin-Wallace College
Criminal Justice Program
Carnegie Hall
Berea, Ohio 44017

Bowling Green State University
Criminal Justice Program
Bowling Green, Ohio 43403

Case Western Reserve University
Center for Criminal Justice
Cleveland, Ohio 44106

Central Ohio Technical College
Div. of Public Service Technologies
University Drive
Newark, Ohio 43055

Clark Technical College
Public Service Dept.
Springfield, Ohio 45501

The Defiance College
Criminal Justice Dept.
701 N. Clinton St.
Defiance, Ohio 43512

Hocking Technical College
Criminal Justice Center
Nelsonville, Ohio 45764

Kent State University
Criminal Justice Studies
6000 Frank Road N.W.
Canton, Ohio 44720

Lakeland Community College
Div. of Social Sciences and Public
   Service Programs
Mentor, Ohio 44060

Lorain County Community
   College
1005 N. Abbe Rd.
Elyria, Ohio 44035

Miami University at Hamilton
Criminal Justice Studies
Hamilton, Ohio 45011

Michael J. Owens Technical
   College
Dept. of Criminal Justice
   Administration
Caller No. 10,000
Oregon Rd.
Toledo, Ohio 43699

Muskingum Area Technical
   College
1555 Newark Rd.
Zanesville, Ohio 43701

North Central Technical College
Law Enforcement Program
Mansfield, Ohio 44901

Ohio Dominican College
Political Science Dept.
1216 Sunbury Rd.
Columbus, Ohio 43219

Ohio University
Athens, Ohio 45701

Sinclair Community College
Criminal Justice Dept.
Dayton, Ohio 45402

Terra Technical College
Public Service Technologies
1220 Cedar St.
Fremont, Ohio 43420

Tiffin University
155 Miami St.
Tiffin, Ohio 44883

University of Cincinnati
Criminal Justice Program
321 French Hall #108
Cincinnati, Ohio 45221

The University of Dayton
Criminal Justice Program
Miriam Hall
Office #818
Dayton, Ohio 45469

Xavier University
Criminal Justice Dept.
Cincinnati, Ohio 45207

Youngstown State University
Dept. of Criminal Justice
Youngstown, Ohio 44555

Oklahoma

Carl Albert Junior College
Criminal Justice
Poteau, Okla. 74953

Central State University
Criminal Justice Program
Edmond, Okla. 73034

Connors State College
Criminal Justice Dept.
Warner, Okla. 74469

Northeastern State University
Criminal Justice Studies
Tahlequah, Okla. 74464

Northern Oklahoma College
Tonkawa, Okla. 74653

Oklahoma City University
Dept. of Criminal Justice
23rd and Blackwelder
Oklahoma City, Okla. 73106

Oklahoma State University
Dept. of Sociology, or Dept. of Political Science
Stillwater, Okla. 74078

Tulsa Junior College
Police Science
909 South Boston
Tulsa, Okla. 74119

University of Oklahoma
Dept. of Political Science
455 W. Lindsey
Room 205
Norman, Okla. 73019

University of Tulsa
Criminal Justice Studies
600 S. College Ave.
Tulsa, Okla. 74101

Oregon

Blue Mountain Community College
Criminal Justice Program
P.O. Box 100
Pendleton, Ore. 97801

Chemeketa Community College
Criminal Justice Dept.
4000 Lancaster Dr. N.E.
Salem, Ore. 97303

Clackamas Community College
Criminal Justice Dept.
19600 S. Molalla Ave.
Oregon City, Ore. 97045

Clatsop Community College
Criminal Justice Dept.
16th and Jerome St.
Astoria, Ore. 97103

Lane Community College
Criminal Justice Program
4000 E. 30th Ave.
Eugene, Ore. 97405

Linn-Benton Community College
Criminal Justice Dept.
6500 Southwest Pacific Blvd.
Albany, Ore. 97321

Oregon College of Education
Criminal Justice Dept.
345 N. Monmouth
Monmouth, Ore. 97341

Portland Community College
Government Services Dept.
12000 Southwest 49th St.
ST A-6
Portland, Ore. 97219

Portland State University
Administration of Justice Dept.
Portland, Ore. 97207

Southwestern Oregon Community
  College
Public Services Dept.
Coos Bay, Ore. 97420

Pennsylvania

Alvernia College
Criminal Justice Programs
Reading, Pa. 19607

Bucks County Community College
Criminal Justice
Newtown, Pa. 18940

Community College of Allegheny
  County/Allegheny Campus
808 Ridge Ave.
Pittsburgh, Pa. 15212

Community College of Allegheny
  County/Boyce Campus
595 Beatty Rd.
Monroeville, Pa. 15146

Duquesne University
Pittsburgh, Pa. 15282

Edinboro State College
Edinboro, Pa. 16444

Harrisburg Area Community
  College
Public Safety Div.
3300 Cameron St. Rd.
Harrisburg, Pa. 17110

Holy Family College
Criminal Justice Programs
Philadelphia, Pa. 19114

Indiana University of Pennsylvania
Criminology Dept.
Indiana, Pa. 15705

Kutztown State College
Kutztown, Pa. 19530

Lehigh County Community
  College
2370 Main St.
Schnecksville, Pa. 18078

Lycoming College
Criminal Justice
Williamsport, Pa. 17701

Mansfield State College
Dept. of Sociology/Social Work/
  Criminal Justice
Mansfield, Pa. 16933

Mercyhurst College
Criminal Justice Administration
Glenwood Hills
Erie, Pa. 16546

Montgomery County Community
  College
Police Science Administration
  Program
340 DeKalb Pike
Blue Bell, Pa. 19422

Moravian College
Criminal Justice Program
Bethlehem, Pa. 18018

The Pennsylvania State University
Administration of Justice Dept.
S-203 Human Development Bldg.,
  or Dept. of Community Systems
S-203 Human Development Bldg.
University Park, Pa. 16802

St. Joseph's University
54th St. and City Ave.
Philadelphia, Pa. 19131

Temple University
Dept. of Criminal Justice
Philadelphia, Pa. 19122

University of Pittsburgh
Administration of Justice Program
435 Cathedral of Learning
Pittsburgh, Pa. 15260

University of Scranton
Dept. of Sociology/Criminal
  Justice
Scranton, Pa. 18510

West Chester State College
Dept. of Criminal Justice
West Chester, Pa. 19380

Widener University
University College
Room 120
Kapelski Center
Chester, Pa. 19013

York College of Pennsylvania
Criminal Justice
Country Club Rd.
York, Pa. 17405

Rhode Island

Roger Williams College
Ferry Rd.
Bristol, R.I. 02809

South Carolina

Baptist College at Charleston
Criminal Justice Dept.
P.O. Box 10087
Charleston, S.C. 29411

Beaufort Technical College
Criminal Justice Dept.
P.O. Box 1288
Beaufort, S.C. 29902

Florence-Darlington Technical
  College
CRJ Program
Florence, S.C. 29501

Greenville Technical College
Institute of Public Service
  Education
P.O. Box 5616
Station B
Greenville, S.C. 29606

Orangeburg-Calhoun Technical
  College
Criminal Justice Dept.
P.O. Drawer 1767
Orangeburg, S.C. 29115

Piedmont Technical College
Criminal Justice Dept.
P.O. Drawer 1467
Greenwood, S.C. 29646

South Carolina State College
Criminal Justice Program
Orangeburg, S.C. 29107

Trident Technical College/Palmer
  Campus
P.O. Box 10367
Charleston, S.C. 29411

University of South Carolina at
  Aiken
Social and Behavioral Sciences
Aiken, S.C. 29801

University of South Carolina at
  Columbia
College of Criminal Justice
Columbia, S.C. 29208

University of South Carolina at
  Spartanburg
Criminal Justice
Spartanburg, S.C. 29303

South Dakota

Dakota Wesleyan University
Criminal Justice Dept.
Mitchell, S. Dak. 57301

Huron College
Criminal Justice Program
Huron, S. Dak. 57350

Northern State College
Criminal Justice Studies
Aberdeen, S. Dak. 57401

University of South Dakota
Criminal Justice Studies Program
Dakota Hall
Vermillion, S. Dak. 57069

Tennessee

Cleveland State Community
  College
Criminal Justice Dept.
Cleveland, Tenn. 37311

East Tennessee State University
Dept. of Criminal Justice
Johnson City, Tenn. 37601

Middle Tennessee State University
Dept. of Criminal Justice
  Administration
Murfreesboro, Tenn. 37132

Milligan College
Field Work in Human Relations
Box 268
Milligan College, Tenn. 37682

University of Tennessee at
  Chattanooga
Criminal Justice Dept.
Chattanooga, Tenn. 37402

University of Tennessee at Martin
Criminal Justice Program
Dept. of Sociology and
  Anthropology
Martin, Tenn. 38238

Walters State Community College
Dept. of Criminal Justice
Appalachian Highway
Morristown, Tenn. 37814

Texas

Amarillo Junior College
Law Enforcement Dept.
P.O. Box 447
Amarillo, Tex. 79178

American Technological University
Criminal Justice Dept.
P.O. Box 1416
Killeen, Tex. 76540

Blinn College
Div. of Occupational Education
902 College Ave.
Brenham, Tex. 77833

College of the Mainland
Div. of Public Service Careers
8001 Palmer Highway
Texas City, Tex. 77590

Corpus Christi State University
College of Arts and Humanities
6300 Ocean Drive
Corpus Christi, Tex. 78412

East Texas State University
Dept. of Sociology and
 Anthropology
Commerce, Tex. 75428

El Centro College
Police Science
Main and Lamar Sts.
Dallas, Tex. 75202

Galveston College
Law Enforcement Program
4015 Avenue Q
Galveston, Tex. 77550

Henderson County Junior College
Occupational Education
Athens, Tex. 75751

Houston Community College
 System
Criminal Justice Program
4701 Dickson St.
Houston, Tex. 77007

Kilgore College
1100 Broadway
Kilgore, Tex. 75662

Lee College
Police Science Dept.
P.O. Box 818
Baytown, Tex. 77520

McLennan Community College
Law Enforcement Education
1400 College Dr.
Waco, Tex. 76708

Midwestern State University
Criminal Justice Program
Wichita Falls, Tex. 76308

Pan American University
Criminal Justice Program
Edinburg, Tex. 78539

Ranger Junior College
Ranger, Tex. 76470

Saint Edward's University
Criminal Justice Dept.
Div. of Behavioral and Social
 Sciences
3001 S. Congress Ave.
Austin, Tex. 78704

St. Mary's University
Public Justice Research
One Camino Santa Maria
San Antonio, Tex. 78284

Sam Houston State University
Criminal Justice Center
Huntsville, Tex. 77341

San Antonio Community College
Criminal Justice
Dept. of Public Affairs
1300 San Pedro Ave.
San Antonio, Tex. 78284

San Jacinto College
Law Enforcement Dept.
8060 Spencer Highway
Pasadena, Tex. 77505

South Plains College
Criminal Justice Div.
Law Enforcement Technology
Levelland, Tex. 79336

Southern Methodist University
Criminal Justice Dept.
210 Hyer Hall
Dallas, Tex. 75275

Southwest Texas State University
Dept. of Criminal Justice
San Marcos, Tex. 78666

Stephen F. Austin State University
Criminal Justice Program
School of Applied Arts and
  Sciences
P.O. Box 6178
Nacogdoches, Tex. 75962

Sul Ross State University
Criminal Justice Dept.
Alpine, Tex. 79830

Tarrant County Junior College/
  Northeast Campus
Criminal Justice Program
828 Harwood Rd.
Hurst, Tex. 76053

Temple Junior College
Vocational/Technical Div.
2600 South 1st
Temple, Tex. 76501

Texarkana Community College
Law Enforcement Administration
2500 North Robison Rd.
Texarkana, Tex. 75501

Texas Woman's University
Criminal Justice Program
P.O. Box 23974
University Station
Denton, Tex. 76204

University of Houston at Clear
  Lake City
Programs in Public Affairs
2700 Bay Area Blvd.
Houston, Tex. 77058

University of Texas at Arlington
Criminal Justice Programs
Institute of Urban Studies
Arlington, Tex. 76019

University of Texas at Tyler
Dept. of Criminal Justice
Tyler, Tex. 75701

Western Texas College
Law Enforcement Dept.
Snyder, Tex. 79549

Utah

Weber State College
Corrections and Law Enforcement
  Education Program
3750 Harrison Blvd.
Ogden, Utah 84408

Virgin Islands

College of the Virgin Islands
Social Sciences Div.
St. Croix
U.S. Virgin Islands 00850

Virginia

Central Virginia Community
  College
Social Science Div.
Lynchburg, Va. 24502

Dabney S. Lancaster Community
  College
Route 60 W.
Clifton Forge, Va. 24422

Ferrum College
Social Work Program
Ferrum, Va. 24088

J. Sargeant Reynolds Community
  College
Administration of Justice Programs
P.O. Box 12084
Richmond, Va. 23241

New River Community College
Administration of Justice
Dublin, Va. 24084

Northern Virginia Community
  College
Administration of Justice
8333 Little River Turnpike
Annandale, Va. 22003

Northern Virginia Community
  College/Woodbridge
Administration of Justice
15200 Smoketown Rd.
Woodbridge, Va. 22191

Radford University
Radford, Va. 24142

Roanoke College
Dept. of History/Political
  Science/Sociology
Salem, Va. 24153

Thomas Nelson Community
  College
Criminal Justice Dept.
P.O. Box 9407
Hampton, Va. 23670

Virginia Commonwealth
  University
Dept. of Administration of Justice
  and Public Safety
901 W. Franklin St.
Richmond, Va. 23284

Virginia Highlands Community
  College
Administration of Justice
Abingdon, Va. 24210

Virginia Western Community
  College
Administration of Justice
3095 Colonial Ave. SW
Roanoke, Va. 24015

Washington

Bellevue Community College
Administration of Criminal Justice
  Program
Bellevue, Wash. 98007

Central Washington University
Program in Law and Justice
Ellensburg, Wash. 98926

Centralia Community College
P.O. Box 639
Centralia, Wash. 98531

City College
Legal Program
Lyon Bldg.
Seattle, Wash. 98104

Eastern Washington University
Criminal Justice
Cheney, Wash. 99004

Everett Community College
Criminal Justice Dept.
801 Wetmore Ave.
Everett, Wash. 98201

Gonzaga University
Criminal Justice Program
Sociology Dept.
Spokane, Wash. 99258

Grays Harbor College
Aberdeen, Wash. 98520

Green River Community College
Criminal Justice
12401 Southeast 320th St.
Auburn, Wash. 98002

Highline Community College
Administration of Justice Program
Midway, Wash. 98031

Olympic College
Div. of Social Sciences and Service
  Occupations
16th and Chester
Bremerton, Wash. 98310

Pacific Lutheran University
Div. of Social Sciences
Tacoma, Wash. 98447

Peninsula College
1502 E. Lauridsen Blvd.
Port Angeles, Wash. 98362

Shoreline Community College
Criminal Justice Education
  Program
16101 Greenwood Ave. N.
Seattle, Wash. 98133

University of Washington
Dept. of Sociology DK-40,
  or Dept. of Political Science
  DO-30
Seattle, Wash. 98195

Washington State University
Dept. of Criminal Justice
Van Doren Hall 106
Pullman, Wash. 99164

West Virginia

Bluefield State College
Dept. of Criminal Justice
Bluefield, W. Va. 24701

Fairmont State College
Criminal Justice Dept.
Fairmont, W. Va. 26554

Parkersburg Community College
Rt. 5, Box 167A
Parkersburg, W. Va. 26101

Southern West Virginia
  Community College
Criminal Justice Program
Togam, W. Va. 25601

West Virginia Northern
  Community College
Criminal Justice Program
College Square
Wheeling, W. Va. 26003

West Virginia State College
Criminal Justice Dept.
P.O. Box 37
Institute, W. Va 25112

Wisconsin

Edgewood College
Dept. of Social Science
Madison, Wisc. 53711

Gateway Technical Institute
Police Science Program
3520 30th Ave.
Kenosha, Wisc. 53141

Lakeshore Technical Institute
1290 North Ave.
Cleveland, Wisc. 53015

Madison Area Technical College
Public Safety Services
211 N. Carroll St.
Madison, Wisc. 53703

Marquette University
Law Enforcement Dept.
1217 W. Wisconsin Ave.
Milwaukee, Wisc. 53233

Milwaukee Area Technical College
Police Science Dept.
1015 N. 6th St.
Milwaukee, Wisc. 53203

Mount Senario College
Ladysmith, Wisc. 54848

Nicolet College
Dept. of Police Science
Box 518
Rhinelander, Wisc. 54501

University of Wisconsin at
  Eau Claire
Eau Claire, Wisc. 54701

University of Wisconsin at
  Milwaukee
Criminal Justice Program
P.O. Box 786
Milwaukee, Wisc. 53201

University of Wisconsin at
  Oshkosh
Criminal Justice Program
Political Science Dept.
Oshkosh, Wisc. 54901

VTAE District One
Law Enforcement Dept.
Eau Claire, Wisc. 54701

Waukesha County Technical
  Institute
Law Enforcement Dept./Service
  Occupations
800 N. Main St.
Pewaukee, Wisc. 53072

Wyoming

Casper College
Criminal Justice Dept.
Casper, Wyoming 82601

Central Wyoming College
Behavioral Science Div.
Riverton, Wyoming 82501

Eastern Wyoming College
3200 W. C St.
Torrington, Wyoming 82240

Sheridan College
Sheridan, Wyoming 82801

University of Wyoming
Political Science Dept.
Laramie, Wyoming 82071

Jobs Within the Criminal Justice System

FEDERAL JOBS

(For job descriptions, qualifications and additional information, write your nearest regional personnel officer in the department of your choice. The address can be secured by telephoning your nearest Federal Information Center listed under United States Government in the telephone directory. You can also obtain a free packet of information about careers in law enforcement by writing Hattie M. Carrington, Information Coordinator, National Information and Research Center on Women in Policing, Police Foundation, 1909 K St. NW, Suite 400, Washington, D.C. 20006. Additional information can also be obtained by writing National Employment Listing Service, Office of Publications, Criminal Justice Center, Sam Houston State University, Huntsville, Texas 77341.)

Department of Agriculture

U.S. Forest Service: Criminal Investigator
Office of Inspector General: Special Agent

Capitol Police

Police Officers

Central Intelligence Agency

(Inquire directly regarding types of jobs.)

Defense Investigative Service

Special Agent-Trainee

Equal Employment Opportunity Commission

Equal Opportunity Officer

Federal Maritime Commission
General Investigators

Federal Trade Commission
Consumer Protection Specialist, Paralegal Specialist, Research Analyst.

General Accounting Office
Auditor

General Services Administration
Federal Protective Officer, Criminal Investigators

Department of Interior

Bureau of Indian Affairs: Criminal Investigator, Police Officer
Bureau of Land Management: Special Agents
U.S. Fish and Wildlife Service: Special Agents, Special Agents/Pilots
National Park Service: Park Aids, Park Technicians, Park Rangers
United States Park Police: Police Officers

Department of Justice

Drug Enforcement Administration: Special Agents, Compliance Investigators
Federal Bureau of Investigation: Special Agents, Computer Programmer and Computer Systems Analysts, Fingerprint Examiners, Radio Maintenance Technicians, Laboratory Positions
Immigration and Naturalization Service: Criminal Investigator-Trainees, Immigration Inspector-Trainees, Border Patrol Agent-Trainees
United States Marshal's Office: Deputy U.S. Marshals
Federal Bureau of Prisons: Correctional Officers
Federal Probation Officers: (Inquire for information)

Department of Labor
Mine Safety and Health Administration: Federal Mine Inspectors

National Aeronautics and Space Administration
Personnel Security Specialists and Officers, Physical Security Specialists and Officers

National Zoological Park Police
Police Officers

Department of the Navy
Criminal Investigators, Police and Guards

Securities and Exchange Commission
Investigators

United States Postal Service
Postal Inspectors

Department of Treasury
Bureau of Alcohol, Tobacco and Firearms: Inspectors, Special Agents
U.S. Customs Service: Customs Inspectors, Dog Handlers, Import Specialists, Customs Patrol Officers, Customs Pilots, Special Agents
Internal Revenue Service: Internal Revenue Agents, Internal Security Inspectors, Special Agents
U.S. Secret Service: Secret Service Uniformed Division Officers, Special Agents

Other Federal Opportunities in Criminal Justice

(The following employ Investigators and Criminal Investigators and, where noted, offer certain other job opportunities in criminal justice.)

Department of the Air Force: Security Specialists
Department of the Army
Civil Aeronautics Board
Department of Commerce
Consumer Products Safety Commission
Environmental Protection Agency
Federal Communications Commission
Federal Deposit Insurance Corporation: Bank Examiners
Federal Home Loan Bank Board
Food and Drug Administration
Department of Housing and Urban Development
Internal Trade Commission
Office of Personnel Management
Social Security Administration
Department of Transportation
Veterans Administration

STATE, COUNTY AND MUNICIPAL JOBS

(These organizations vary in different locales. For specific information, contact the personnel department within the agency of your choice. For additional information, write for a free packet on careers in law enforcement: Hattie M. Carrington, Information Coordinator, National Information and Research Center on Women in Policing, Police Foundation, 1909 K St. NW, Suite 400, Washington, D.C. 20006. Further information can also be obtained by writing: National Employment Listing Service, Office of Publications, Criminal Justice Center, Sam Houston State University, Huntsville, Texas 77341.)

INDEX

Airport security agent, 113–115
Alcatraz Prison, 74
Alcohol violations, 23
Aliens, illegal, 105–109
Atlanta (Ga.), 113–115

Blankenship, Betty, 7
Blood analysis, 49–51
Border Patrol, 105–110
Border Patrol Academy, 106
Brighton (Colo.), 116–119
Burnside, Clara, 6

Cardiopulmonary resuscitation (CPR), 30, 72
Charlotte (N. Car.), 85–91, 96–101
Chicago (Ill.), 5, 6, 56, 57
Cleveland (Ohio), 8
Coffal, Elizabeth, 7
College courses, 46
  in criminal justice, 28, 125–149
Colorado Law Enforcement Training Academy, 118
Coral reefs, 35–37, 39–41
Correctional institutions
  description of work in, 110–113
  first female officers in, 5
  halfway house, 83–91, 96–101
  public education field officer for, 95
  state director of, 119–122
Crimes, number of, 61

Davenport (Iowa), 57
Demonstrations, federal mounted police at, 66

Detective work, 7, 116–119
Dickinson, Angela, 26
Dilaudid, 15
Drunks, arrest of, 80

Explorer Scouting programs, 28

Federal Aviation Administration (FAA), Air Transportation Security Division of, 113–115
Federal Bureau of Investigation (FBI), 49–61
  Academy (Quantico, Va.), 24–26, 55–56, 71–72, 114
  first female agents of, 7, 54
  laboratory analysis by, 49–52, 54, 61
  number of agents of, by sex, 61
Federal jobs in criminal justice, listed, 150–152
Federal Law Enforcement Center (Glynco, Ga.), 71–74, 77, 82
Fernandez, Valerie, 77
Firearms, federal training in, 72–73
First black female Border Patrol agent, 106
First father-daughter police team, 6–7
First female federal mounted officers, 64
First female state troopers, 7
First female jailer, 5
First female prison matron, 5
First policewomen, 3–6
Florida Marine Patrol, 29–37, 42–48
Forensic science, 50

Gateway National Recreation Area, 66

153

BREAKTHROUGH: Women in Law Enforcement

Glynco (Ga.) Federal Law Enforcement Training Center, 71–74, 77, 82
Golden Gate National Recreational Area, 65, 66, 74–79
Guzman, Virginia Quintana, 116–119

Halfway house, 83–91, 96–101
Henrico County (Va.), 5
Heroin, 23
Higgins, Maureen Anne, 49–61
"Hill Street Blues," 26
Hostages, 82

Indianapolis (Ind.), 6, 7
Information on women in policing, where to get, 152
International Association of Police Chiefs, 119

Johnson, Everene Cooper, 6
Juveniles, police rap sessions with, 117–118

Kandler, Elizabeth Aytes (Cookie), 83–101
Karansky, Priscilla Pepper, 63–82
Kilroy, Karen, 8

Lindsey, Mary, 5
Los Angeles (Calif.), 3–5

McAllen (Tex.), 105–106
McCarthy, Alice, 6
McNamara, Rae Hassell, 119–122
Marijuana, 13, 23, 32
Marine patrol, 29–37, 42–48
Married police officers, 22, 24–27
Massachusetts, 7
Mentors, 70, 81
Miami (Fla.), 7
Milwaukee (Wisc.), 56
Morris, Kathryn Harper, 113–115
Mounted police, federal, 64–65, 71, 77–79
Murder
   laboratory analysis in, 49–51
   statistics on, 61

Narcotics cases, 10–19, 23–24, 27, 32–35
Nashville (Tenn.), 19–24, 26
New York City, 5, 66, 77
North Carolina Director of Prisons, 119–122

Owens, Mary, 5

Parade magazine, 119
Patrol duty, women on, 7–8, 23
   marine patrol, 29–37, 42–48
Pence, Donna Marie, 10–28
Pitts, Lavelle, 34
Police cadet programs, 28
"Police Woman" (TV series), 26
Portland (Ore.), 5
Prisons, *see* Correctional institutions
Probation-parole officer, 95
Prostitution, 17
Purolator heist, 57

Quaalude, 10–12
Quantico (Va.), FBI Academy in, 24–26, 55–56, 71–72, 114

Raleigh (N. Car.), 120
Rape, statistics on, 61
Rape crisis center, 20
Rio Grande, 105, 106

Salaries, women's vs. men's, 26
San Diego (Calif.), 108
San Francisco (Calif.), 65, 66, 74–79
Seattle (Wash.), 9
Secret Service, 7
Security guards, female, 22, 26, 41
Sky-marshal program, 114
Snyder, Tom, "Tomorrow" show of, 20
Sprecher, Jenna Garman, 29–48
Stanton, Susan Marie, 110–113
Statistics on the number of female law-enforcement officers, 5–7, 61
Surveillance, women's excellence at, 60–61

Tennessee Bureau of Investigation, 10–19, 24, 28
Thompson, Beryl A., 9
Trap robbing, 30–31

United States Park Police Mounted Unit, 64–65, 71, 77–79
University Heights (Iowa), 6

Walker, Mark, 29–33
Washington (D.C.), 6–7, 65–66, 77
Wells, Alice Stebbins, 3–5, 7, 9
Winder, Esther, 6
Wives of male officers, 8, 43
Woodard, James, 121